ON THE SOIL OF ISRAEL

D1108681

YAAKOV MORRIS

On the Soil
of Israel

AMERICANS AND CANADIANS IN AGRICULTURE

PUBLISHED BY THE ASSOCIATION OF
AMERICANS AND CANADIANS IN ISRAEL

The Association of Americans and Canadians in Israel
Rehov Hayarkon 53a, Tel Aviv, Israel.

Tel Aviv, 1965

Cover, layout and illustrations by Reuven Berman.
Printed at the Davar Press.

FOREWORD

The Jews of the United States and Canada number over half of the Jews in the world, excluding Israel. It is consequently self-evident that Israel considers them a most important potential factor in the development of the State. Indeed, since we assume that the future of the Jews as a people is now once again centered in Israel, it is inconceivable that over half of our people in the diaspora should not play a major role in the settlement and upbuilding of its national homeland. This is all the more so because the three million additional Jews who live in Soviet Russia are prevented from taking their part in our national endeavour.

With this in mind, Mr. Morris portrays the participation of American Jews in this great adventure, pointing out their achievements, difficulties, and problems; and examines the reasons for the failure of many of them to strike roots in the country. His conclusion is that as a group they have as yet failed to contribute anything like their share to the task, whilst as individuals they have demonstrated conclusively that it is possible for American Jews to be integrated in the life of the country and to find an honoured place in its public life.

We have here not an outpouring of emotional appreciation, but a factual appraisal of American Jewish efforts in Israel, and in Palestine before the establishment of the State.

There are many interesting historical facts heretofore little known, such as American Jewish colonisation endeavours as early as 100 years ago. American Jews were among the founders of the oldest agricultural settlements and of the Moshavei Ovdim and many to this day are active in the kibbutz movement.

There is ample evidence that there are no basic reasonable grounds which preclude a large immigration of American Jews into Israel, and that the real reason for the comparatively negligible number of American Jews who have come to settle in the country is simply their unwillingness to do so.

This severe but sad stricture of the Zionist movement in America cannot be gainsaid, but this situation can still be remedied.

The importance of a greatly increased immigration of American Jews lies not merely in the numbers they could add to Israel's population. By their education, training, experience and way of life in America, during many decades, they have acquired qualities, knowledge, technical skills, administrative ability and a deep-seated appreciation of the democratic way of life. All these attributes would contribute to the economic development of the country, particularly in the industrial, commercial, building and scientific spheres, and also to the advancement of the democratic institutions of the State. Such a contribution could be of great importance to the State. It could help ensure that Israel will be the kind of state its founders and friends visualised, a state based on principles of social justice, the rule of law, equality of opportunity and genuine democracy.

The book is a challenge to American Jewry. One can only hope they will be prepared to take up and meet the challenge with some measure of success.

Dov Joseph

INTRODUCTION

Despite popular opinion, American pioneer history in Israel did not begin with either Avichail or Ein Hashofet. Nor were Habonim, Hashomer Hatzair and Hashomer Hadati-Bnei Akiva in the United States and Canada the first movements to send settlers to Palestine. There were earlier and repeated attempts, however sporadic, to form movements and found villages. In many ways they were even more heroic because they began without backing either in America or in the National Home.

The lone individual or tiny groups that set sail from New York for a land still dominated by the Ottoman Turks, a land still without geo-political identity, had more than daring or determination. They were the sons and daughters of a certain period of American Jewish history. To most of them the United States was but a way-station on the road to Zion. Born in Czarist Russia, Poland, Rumania or the Baltic states, steeped in the culture and traditions of Eastern European Jewry, they were Zionists in transit. America was an episode, however short or long, in their exile from their Promised Land.

Alive in them were the same revolutionary social and national ideals that motivated the Jewish student youth from Russia who arrived in Palestine in 1881-82 under the banner of the Bilu or those who came from Poland and Russia in the days of the famous Second Aliya from 1904 to 1920. The ideologies they brought with them to America had little application to life in that country. They were confined to the Jewish expatriates who had left Europe behind them but had not yet found a place in a new American culture.

Even as American Zionist pioneer history began, with the formation of continuous Zionist youth movements and the establishment of lasting villages in Palestine itself, the first chapter of this history was written by such "expatriates" — by people who lived in a type of no-man's land between Eastern Europe, America and Palestine. In those days, which historians choose to describe as the period of the "melting pot" in America, the common language of the East Side of New York was Yiddish, and the most frequent occupation was tailoring. Continuing the same traditions, the ideological battles fought in the East European ghettos still prevailed around Delancey Street and the other crowded immigrant districts of major American cities.

Palestine at the time, was in many ways no less a "melting pot". The newcomers brought with them ideologies of every shade in the political spectrum. While all were resolved to build Zion, opinions and deeds clashed sharply as to how the future Jewish State was to be built. Most characteristic of these differences was the contrast between the farmers of the Bilu period and the newcomers of the Second Aliya who arrived two decades later. The Zionist Organization itself, founded in 1897, had only begun its settlement activities and these were in their most formative and experimental stages.

In some respects, it was easy for America's first Zionist pioneers to leave for Palestine. Having no roots in the new American culture, they could abandon it with few qualms. Awaiting them was a sparsely-settled land, with swamps and deserts. Whatever they achieved there would be of their own invention, would be their own distinctive contribution. They could fashion villages according to their own social ideals, found a culture in accordance with their ideas. That, too, was an attraction greater than adjusting to established patterns.

Yet, with all the expatriate nature of their lives in the United States, these first American settlers in Palestine brought with them a quality distinctly their own. Few Israelis are today aware that as early as 1872, long before Degania, "Mother of the Collectives", started in 1910, a settler named Simon Berman and 24 other Americans farmed their land collectively just outside Jerusalem.

This inventiveness is distinctly an American tradition, although certainly not exclusively so. It stems from the fact that when the United States itself was formed it inherited no feudal traditions or peasantry. Its start in agriculture was completely new.

This, certainly, was part of the tradition of Berman and so was their independence, their freedom of spirit. It may be detected today even among the apparently "standard" collective and cooperative villages built long after them by American settlers in Israel. On closer examination, they reveal some interesting variations. Such, for example, is the case of Gesher Haziv, on the northern Coastal Plain, where — unlike the practice in most other collectives — parents and children live together in family housing units. Even the bathtub brought to the Northern Sharon by the Friedlander family in 1927 was then a revolution in the entire area.

To inventiveness must be added know-how, the American aptitude for organization and technical efficiency. Wherever pioneers from that country have founded villages or joined others already started, these attributes may be discerned. Another distinctive attribute has been open-mindedness, a refusal to accept dogma and tradition mechanically, an ability to listen to an opposite or differing point of view.

Perhaps most important of all is that American pioneering in Israel, from its sporadic, unorganized beginnings to the continuous movement be-

tween the 1920's and today, has been one of free
choice, not of compulsion. No one expelled these
pioneers from America or refused to let them in
elsewhere. Neither pauperization nor antisemitism
caused them to leave that country, nor were they
particularly courted or welcomed in Palestine.
In fact most were first received with incredulity
and often met with the question: "Why did you
come — what are you doing here?"

This is their strength — it is also their weakness. They have been propelled by spiritual forces
primarily. On the other hand, as a cynic once put
it, "there is no greater patriotism than that of
no alternative". To the American, there is always
the road back; his bridges have not finally been
burned. When he withstands hardships and remains
steadfast as an Israeli pioneer, the American is
most admired. At times, when he gives up in the
face of a gruelling test, he is often envied. In both
situations there is little anonymity, the spotlight
is harsh.

To the Israeli in general, the American pioneer
has always been difficult to understand. Particularly since the 1930's, after Hitler's rise to power
in Europe, Israel has been receiving the remnants
of broken Jewish communities, people often ill in
body and mind. Once again, it has become difficult to accept the idea that people may come to
Israel for positive reasons, not simply seeking a
haven but out of the desire to participate in the
building of a national culture. This sceptical
materialist and determinist viewpoint is not merely

the product of prolonged philanthropy; it also reflects a post-State decline of Israel's own idealism. If it has been difficult for the Israeli to understand American pioneers in Israel, it has been no less so for the majority of American Jews. Affluent as they have become, they resist accepting the fact that there are people for whom affluence is no end or meaning to human existence. This, too, is materialism and determinism. Opposition in the early thirties often found rationalized expression when even Zionists queried the right of an American youngster to take the place of a European refugee in the British-certificated entry queue for Palestine. And when the gates of Zion finally were forced wide open in 1948 with the foundation of an independent Jewish State, departure for Israel was often mistakenly confused with a rejection of America.

The fact is that pioneer immigration of Americans to Israel is no rejection of the United States. The most successful pioneers are those most adjusted to both countries. The pioneer carries with him to Israel an unending love of all that is positive in America. He has remained in Israel because he is a Jew who seeks, like the original American, to build a new home of his own. The force that draws him is magnetically positive, it is the adventure of building a new Jewish culture.

In this respect the pioneers from America today differ little from those who reached Palestine during the 19th century. What has changed in the meantime is American Jewry. The Jews of that country in its present stage of "cultural pluralism" feel sufficiently rooted so as not to fear assertion of their positive differences from the rest of the population. Logically, they have not yet accepted the fact that these differences may be such as to impel young Americans ultimately to seek an even greater Jewishness in a Jewish State.

A dialogue between American searchers and Israeli creators of a new and meaningful Jewish culture and ethos can be the only true bridge between the best of the youth of these two free Jewries of the contemporary world. The American pioneer in Israel is at the core of this dialogue.

CHAPTER I

First Attempts

There are many roads for the Jew to Zion. From America, the road has always been that of the spirit, as a century of history suggests. The first to walk it, strangely enough, was not a Jew, but a Christian who sought Judaism. His name, when the journey began, was Warder Cresson, first United States Consul to be accredited to the Turkish Court. His area of jurisdiction, proposed by the State Department in 1844, was "All the Holy Land" and the following year he took up residence in Jerusalem. To say the least, the terms of reference were obscure, as the "Holy Land" then had neither geographic nor political definition. It was part of the Syrian Pashalik that included Syria and the areas today called Jordan and Israel.

The following year Warder Cresson changed both his name and faith. He became a Jew called Michael Boaz Israel. On the outskirts of Jerusalem he founded an agricultural settlement called "God's Vineyard". His goal was nothing less than "the migration of all Jews as desire to settle in the land given by the Almighty in covenant to Abraham and his seed forever..." After distributing pamphlets in Europe and America stating this aim, Michael Boaz Israel was joined within four years by 200 Americans, at least 52 of them Jews. The others were either converts to Judaism or Protestants who believed in Zionism.

Little more is known of the fate of Michael Boaz Israel or the settlement "God's Vineyard". Initially, it was a success. Its produce was sold in the markets of Hebron and Jericho. Israel himself married a New York Jewish girl in 1860 and settled permanently in Jerusalem. His third son, it is recorded, studied in an Orthodox seminary there. When and why his settlement broke up, and what happened to its members remains a mystery.

There is more information about the second American pioneer attempt, led by young Simon Berman. He was among the first Polish immigrants to America in 1852 and, unlike most Jewish newcomers at that time, he headed west and became a farmer. He worked his land successfully until 1869, sold his farm and boarded a ship in New York for Jaffa. Berman took a full year to find suitable land for settlement off the Jaffa highway, and built on it three houses, a cowshed and a warehouse. In 1871 he sowed his first crops. A signboard outside his farm announced: "The Holy Land Settlement Society".

Before long, it became a "society" in more than just name. Twenty-four Americans joined

him and the farm began to prosper. Its crops
flourished and it had a large dairy. Berman, however, was far from satisfied. Each day except on
the Sabbath, he traveled from Jaffa to Jerusalem
in his donkey-drawn cart to seek further recruits,
and soon he succeeded in attracting more than
eighty additional members, men and women. If
reports about the Berman experiment are accurate,
then not Degania in 1910 but "The Holy Land
Settlement Society" forty years earlier was
the first collective settlement in modern Palestine.
According to these reports, although Berman and
his American friends provided all the capital for
the farm, its equipment and livestock, everything
belonged collectively to the group. The members
elected their management committees, and, most
revolutionary at the time, every woman in the
community had equal voting rights with the men.
The group also elected a village **muchtar** (mayor
or headman) and a Rabbi.

Because of its radical ideas, the settlement
became the target of widespread opposition and
attack. The center of the opposition was Jerusalem, where Berman had made the most converts
to his projects and found most of his new recruits.
The Rabbis there, supported by charity contributions from abroad, soon became jealous of Berman's growing financial aid from the U. S. A.
Moreover, their pupils were becoming distract-
ed from their studies by the stories they heard
of this experiment by men to "establish the King-
dom of God on earth", and the Rabbis accused

the Americans of heresy in seeking to speed the
redemption which had to come in God's own
good time. Many members of the settlement,
shocked to find themselves accused of "godless-
ness", left it. Berman recorded his misfortunes
in a booklet entitled "The Wanderings of Simon".

Berman then went to Europe. In Poland he
met Rabbi Zvi Hirsch Kalischer and other leaders
of the "Hovevei Zion" (Lovers of Zion) movement
which preceded the Zionist Organization. It appears that he only won the moral support of Kalischer and the movement when he convinced them
of his plans for a great society of Jewish farmers
who would work the soil together in Palestine,
"with faith and in complete equality".

Berman returned to Palestine in 1881, a disappointed man. He died only a few weeks before
the first pioneers of the Russian Bilu society
arrived in the country. According to Pinchas E.
Lapide, in "A Century of U.S. Aliya", they arrived
with (Berman's) book in their hands and his
dream in their hearts... to work the broad land
of Israel properly..."

It is estimated that before the 19th century
had ended several thousand young Americans tried
their hand at pioneering in Palestine. In his book
"Rebirth and Destiny of Israel", David Ben-
Gurion notes: "Our agricultural work began some
seventy years before the State. The finest
pioneers of Eastern Jewry, then intact, made it
possible. Thousands of American Jews were among
them." Famous early villages such as Hadera,

Gedera and Rosh Pina counted Americans among
their founders. It is known, for example, that in
1889 some 40 American students at a Rabbinical
seminary in the Old City of Jerusalem left to join
early agricultural villages in different parts of
the country.

In 1897, the year that the World Zionist
Organization was founded in Europe by Theodor
Herzl, a Zionist Federation was formed in America. Its initial membership was 6,000. Six years
later Russian immigrants to the United States
launched the Techia (Renaissance) organization
and constituted the majority of its 1,200 members. In 1904 a number of Techia "activists", im-
patient about the interminable policy discussions
as to how all Palestine could be acquired, decided
to take direct steps themselves to regain the land.
In a small office in New York one night they
decided to found Hechalutz.

The following summer, at its 1905 conference,
the 400 members of Hechalutz proclaimed: "Our
name, Hechalutz, expresses the essence of our
ideology. We are the vanguard of our people in
its struggle for regeneration in its homeland. Our
outlook and our convictions require no sanction
of theory. We are children of the Jewish nation.
Our close ties with it are natural as those of a
family. Only abnormal people lack national consciousness or find expression for it in chauvinism."

Hechalutz (whose name means "pioneer") was
the first Zionist youth organization of its kind,
not only in the United States but in the world.

It preceded the birth of Hechalutz in Poland and
Russia by more than a decade and provided the
framework for all young Zionists pledged to
devote their own lives to pioneer work in Palestine, regardless of individual political or ideological concepts. A small group of the movement decided to train itself for settlement on the land
and twelve of its members enrolled at the
Woodbine, New Jersey, Agricultural School in
the year 1908.

One of the founding members of Hechalutz,
and a leader of the Woodbine group, was Russian-
born Eliezer Yoffe. Despite the anti-Zionist nature
of the school, meetings were organized and a bi-
monthly was published. Soon, young people outside
the school were contacted, and a gathering was
held in Philadelphia where the organization Haikar
Hatzair — Young Farmer — was launched. Soon
after, it was decided that Eliezer Yoffe should
sail for Palestine to seek a suitable settlement
project there for the group. Meanwhile, on graduation, the other members began additional agricultural training in specialized farm branches.

In 1911, Yoffe arrived in Kinneret, a primitive
farm settlement which straddled the Jordan River.
The place was rugged by any standards. In winter
its land was flooded as the river overflowed its
banks. The few buildings were in ruins, rain poured
through their tumbledown walls. Summer heat
opened the cracks in them even more. Farmland
was strewn with stones and boulders, projecting
rocks had to be blasted to clear a way for any

plough. A neighboring and hostile tribe of nomads repeatedly ambushed the Kinneret farmers,
burning their crops and pillaging.

Various unsuccessful experiments had been
made by others at the Kinneret farm before Yoffe
came to settle a group of permanent workers
there. All had failed administratively because of
the relations between manager and hired hands.
The manager had been appointed by the Palestine Office of the Jewish National Fund which
had acquired the Kinneret land. The workers
consisted of new Jewish immigrants who had
come to the country imbued with the ideals of
individual equality and social justice that had
motivated the Russian revolutionaries of 1905.
When the clash between management and workers occurred at Kinneret, the Palestine Office
sought a different kind of set-up for its farm.

Dr. Arthur Ruppin, German-born and world
famous Jewish sociologist, then headed the Palestine Office. He was progressive, even radical,
and he was ready for both experiment and innovation, however daring. His new plan for Kinneret
was completely revolutionary. He divided the
farm land of the settlement and offered it
to two groups. The part situated on the east bank
of the Jordan was leased to a small group of
workers who had lived as a collective in Hadera.

There, as hired hands, they had pooled their
income, shared expenses, taken their food in a
communal dining hut. The offer of land by Ruppin gave them the opportunity of attempting to

develop their collectivism further and create a
new type of village. They moved to Kinneret in
1910; their settlement became Degania.

Eliezer Yoffe was offered the Kinneret land on
the west bank of the Jordan for his American
group, Haikar Hatzair. He signed a contract with
Dr. Ruppin whereby the Americans would take
over their part of the farm in October 1912 for
one year. As in the case of the Romni group
which started Degania, the Americans undertook
to share any profits with the Palestine office. If
losses were to be incurred, however, the Americans
who had funds of their own would bear them.

By October 1912 only three other members of
the Haikar Hatzair group had joined Yoffe at Kinneret. Yoffe himself, during the year on the farm,
had already established his reputation as a skilled
and determined farmer. Among the three new
arrivals was Berele Klei, a California-trained agri-
culturist, who had specialized in poultry breeding.
He, too, soon earned fame as a skilled planner
and scientific farmer among the workers who had
remained on the farm after the manager left. He
was known as "the American". The remaining
eight members of the American group stayed in
the United States.

Yoffe, the three Americans, and approximately
25 other workers ended the year of contract with
financial loss. Their land was markedly inferior to
that worked by the founders of Degania, its wheat
yield for example was substantially less. Although
his farm had been cultivated as a single economic

unit, on the same lines as that on the east bank
of the river, Yoffe came to an entirely different
conclusion from that reached by the Degania settlers. Production, he maintained, could be increased
if the land were   sub-divided   into   individual
farm units. The Palestine Office, however, would
not agree to his proposal and handed over the
farm on the west bank to a group of workers will-
ing to develop it on the same collective lines as
Degania.

Six years later Eliezer Yoffe issued a pamphlet
entitled "Yissud Moshvei Ovdim" ("The Establishment   of   Smallholders'   Co-operative   Villages"),
outlining the blueprint for the Israel moshav, today
the   most   popular   type   of   agricultural   village
in the country. He criticized sharply the private
and collective villages of the time and his opinions
became the basis of sharp and continuous controversy among   the   rural   population   then   in
the country. Whilst in 1912 his ideas had been
premature, by 1919 they were welcomed enthu-
siastically as an alternative to the collective, prom-
ising no less efficiency in agricultural settlement and group life.

It was not until 1921, however, that his ideas
were first put to the test. In that year Nahalal,
the first moshav, was founded and among its
members was a group of the original settlers of
Degania, headed by Shmuel Dayan. In the spring
of that year Yoffe had presented to the Zionist
authorities on behalf of Nahalal's settlers a proposal for the lease of 2,000 acres for the settle-

ment of 80 families. They would engage in mixed farming as smallholders, produce all their own clothing, market their surplus produce cooperatively, and purchase the manufactured goods they required the same way. The plan was passed on to Ruppin who agreed that each family would obtain 25 acres. Hence, in 1921, the Nahalal group commenced draining the marshes of the Jezreel Valley.

According to the book "Arise and Build — the Story of American Habonim" (Page 27), edited by David Breslau, developments in America after Yoffe's departure in 1911 were rapid. "Two leaders of Palestinian Jewry, David Ben-Gurion and Itzchak Ben-Zvi, arrived in 1915. They zealously started a campaign to organize Hechalutz, to prepare a reserve of pioneers for Palestine when hostilities ceased. About 150 young men signed up. They began to study Hebrew and to work on farms. Many subsequently joined the Jewish Legion; and, of these, some remained permanently in Palestine."

Among the Legionnaires was Sam Friedlander and the founders of the first successful American village in Israel, the moshav Avichail.

CHAPTER II

History Begins with Sam

The permanent story starts with Sam, not "Uncle", but "Father" of lasting American pioneer settlement in Israel. Like many others, he changed his family name when the Jewish State arose, and became Dror in place of Friedlander. But it is as Friedlander that the village of Avichail will always know him, as will many of Israel's founders. So too, will most immigrants who came from the United States. Simply, the fate of a legend, is that it cannot change its name, and Sam Friedlander is nothing less.

At the Henrietta Szold Award Dinner held as part of the 1963 Annual Convention of the Association of Americans and Canadians in Israel, Sam and Leah Dror were among the guests honored for their many years on the land.

At 75, Sam is still sharp and vigorous. The dart and shine of his small black eyes betray mischief, humor and intelligence. The beetling, unruly eyebrows and high cheek bones give Sam's face the look of the proverbial leprechaun. His trunk is slightly stooped, and with his silver-topped foliage Friedlander brings to mind the gnarl and stubbornness of an olive tree. Few trees, of any variety, have borne such fruit. In quality and quantity, its yields has been prodigious since it first sank unshakable roots into sandy and eroded soil.

The eroded soil was in the northern Sharon Plain where nothing existed between Ben Ami's sandy Natanya and Smilansky's marshy Hadera. In this void Friedlander built the first proper house and installed in it his wife and three tiny children. If atmosphere was needed to underline his role as a rugged pioneer, it was supplied by 200 hostile Bedouin whose rough black tents peppered the dun of the plain. Here on this far away east Mediterranean shore, was a fitting setting for a genuine Westerner. As Sam recalls: "When the Bedouin were uprooting my trees, I went out with my rifle. Lily stayed home with a .45 automatic and guarded the children."

Sam, defending his lone homestead in what he calls "no man's land", reenacted in the twenties of this century another poignant piece of American pioneer history. The traffic of Jews from the bondage and persecution of Occident and Orient that reached Sam's private piece of shore in little boats may well be likened to the "underground railroad" of slaves, escaping from the southern plantations and following the north star. Curiously enough, the code song of the American underground railroad was "The Old Ship of Zion", and it was the signal that no bloodhounds were around. The ship had indeed "landed

many a thousand" and "would land many more", as
the slave song said.   Sam picked up the melody when
he brought the "new ships of Zion" ashore, each
a tiny rowboat or sailing vessel, crammed with
Jewish fugitives. The Friedlander house, a valiant
stockade, was a proud Middle East echo of John
Brown's station.

Sam's station had a bathtub, probably the first
in the land. This, too, was a valued American
interpenetration of Israel history. It certainly de-
serves a word. Lily had insisted on bringing it as
her sole condition when she agreed to leave the
comfort of New Jersey's West Orange for the
rigors of the Sharon plain. Primitive as its arrange-
ments were for heat and water, the bathtub
saved lives. Doctors brought patients to it on
donkey and camel-back from miles around. In
retrospect, the Friedlander bathtub looms large
as a symbol of American pioneering in Israel.
Through it the myriad "ethnic" pattern of this
strident new civilization, rising amid the flies and
dust of a Levantine plain, obtained a further
dimension. The bathtub became an object of pilgrimage, a local Sharon myth. It had more importance then than the supermarkets which today
represent an American invasion into Israel's major
cities. The bathtub was kept filled by the purest
of water from the only sweet well in the region.
That, too, was a Friedlander first. It made the
orange grove possible. It beckoned with sparkling
invitation to the first settlers of Natanya who
otherwise never would have chosen their site.

Through its water flowed hope that Sam's Legionnaire village, Avichail, would one day rise in the
neighborhood.

There are many other facets of Sam. His humor has that unmistakable Yiddish itch to tell
stories against himself. Most of them — and there
is an endless supply — are about how he thought
he was fooling the British when they knew
what he was doing all along. That he kept out
of prison during the underground fight against
the British can be attributed solely to his extraordinary personal relations with many of them.
On their "desert" patrols the Friedlander house
was a shimmering oasis of hospitality. Besides
tea or scotch, beer, or often a solid meal, there
was the proverbial bathtub. His hospitality reached rare heights one night when he threw a
gargantuan party. Scarcely a police officer or
official in the entire district was not invited.
Festivities filled not only the night but continued
well past the dawn.

The party was of course one of the moves
in an endless game of chess played between the
men smuggling in immigrants and the British.
Looking at the crowded, noisy room, Sam thought:
"Literally, the coast is clear." A shipload of 265
young pioneers was supposed to be moving slowly
towards the shore. While the party was on, Sam's
friends were to land them and get them safely
well into the country. As the valuable hours of
darkness ticked by, the Friedlanders got worried.
With dawn the ship was sure to be discovered. By

the time the party broke up, it had still not arrived.
The game of chess that night ended in stalemate.
The "illegals", delayed by storm, did reach the
shore without a covering party two nights later,
and were safely smuggled past the British patrols. The following day a police officer dropped
into the Friedlanders for afternoon tea. "Still landing those illegals?" he asked Lily. "How many
came ashore the night of the party?"

Politics, even in those hectic days, never determined Sam's personal relations. He was fighting
British policy, not individual soldiers and police.
They felt this all the time. Years after the British withdrew, his correspondence with many of
them was voluminous. Some came back later to
a free Israel as his guests. Some, he has since
visited in their English homes. The quality in
Sam that generated so much friendship amid the
battle, and disarmed the British because it was a
quality they cherished too, was tolerance. In many
ways they understood it better than the people of
Sam's own side.

He has an unusual position towards domestic
politics even to this day. "Myself?" he says, "I am
non-party." It is a statement often received, in
Israel's supercharged partisan atmosphere, with
censure as severe as meets an American announcing
he hates baseball. Though he was both friend and
colleague to Katznelson and Golomb, and has been
close to Ben Gurion for years, he also favored
the interment of Jabotinsky's bones in the reborn
State.

Only three words are needed to sum up Sam's approach : "Intolerant of intolerance". Tolerance, in Sam, is not merely a part of a general Western tradition. His military training no doubt helped to develop his independent stand, which puts the emphasis on national interests above purely partisan ones.

Sam's career as a soldier began in 1917 because he was a conscious Jew. Most of Europe was locked in war. When Britain issued the Balfour Declaration*, Sam Friedlander, like thousands of others, felt the war was his, even though America was not yet involved. As a volunteer, he crossed the Canadian frontier to train for battle at Windsor, Nova Scotia. Here, battalions of a Jewish Legion were being assembled to fight under the British flag. Their special war aim was to drive the Turks out of Palestine and open its doors for the Jewish return. Sam was in good company. In a neighboring battalion of the same Legion were Ben-Gurion and Itzchak Ben-Zvi. In Sam's unit was a Palestinian named Avram Friedman. Their friendship was both instant and fateful.

Avram, an agricultural student at Berkeley, California, was the son of early pioneer parents. They had established the modern Jewish village of Rosh Pina in Upper Galilee. He joined the Legion to fight for his home. Both men, while still in Windsor, shared the belief that a land worth fighting for was worth settling. Between them

* On November 2, 1917.

the idea emerged that after the war the Legionnaires should be kept together, and no better way
could be found to achieve this than a special
project of their own in the post-war Jewish re-
construction of Palestine. More specifically, they
set their goal as the establishment of a Legionnaire village, and when the fighting ended each
assumed a clear task. Avram, as the trained agronomist, would remain in Palestine to seek suitable land. Sam, a builder with experience in finance
in America, would return there to raise the money
to purchase it.

Nothing less than the offer of a complete Arab
village crossed the Mediterranean and Atlantic
from Avram to Sam. Its location was in the Valley of Jezreel, famed Esdraelon of history and
the future breadbasket of Israel. It was an exci-
ting proposal and Sam hastened to raise the dollars
for a cash deposit. However, by the time the
money reached Avram the option was lost
and the search again proceeded. It finally ended
when a stretch to the north of the Sharon Plain
was offered and agronomist Avram was assured
that its sandy soil was suitable for citriculture.
Six years had elapsed since the two men had been
demobilized and first set about realizing their
plan.

When the purchase was made in 1926, Sam
began urging ex-Legionnaires from the U. S.
to buy sections of land and prepare to settle
on them. Avram did likewise among the Legionnaires who had chosen to remain in Palestine.

Altogether some 152 acres had been acquired,
registered at Tulkarm, the administrative center
of the British Mandatory government, and the
usual baksheesh paid. The following year Sam
set sail to inspect the site. When he arrived,
even his incurable optimism must have been
shaken. The site was a stretch of arid void. It was
covered by dust and sand. The largest question-
mark was whether water could be found any-
where underneath it. All around were the black,
goatskin tents of the feckless Bedouin who both
resented the intrusion and welcomed it as providing
possible prey. Northwards, where the sand ended,
began the green stench of the Hadera swamp.

The turning-point in the fate of Avram and Sam,
of the Legion project, and ultimately of the
entire area came when they struck water, more
precious to them than diamonds. It was clean
and pure and abundant. It attracted the very first
settlers of what was to become the resort town
of Natanya who were then scouring the neighborhood for a suitable settlement site. The first
pipes were brought forty miles from the railway
station at Tulkarm on the backs of mules and
camels. The famous orange grove — Pardess
Hagedud, (Orchard of the Legion) — was begun. Then, it was the first, though modest step-
ping-stone towards the establishment of the Legion village. It was the place where the first
eight Legionnaire families gathered together and
developed a cooperative project. When the others
came, there were enough for a village.

The first real building to rise at the grove was the four-roomed house of Sam Friedlander. In West Orange, building had been his profession, and Sam — with the hired help of some of the Bedouin — soon had his house ready for Lily and his three small daughters. There is little need to emphasize the severity of the challenge, the daring of the Friedlander family. In their isolation, they called the place "no man's land".

Sam gave Natanya's first settlers employment, clearing the land and planting the saplings of the Legionnaires' grove: "I paid them 80 piastres per day, including the use of their mules," he now reflects with a chuckle, and he still has the carefully kept accounts of those days to prove it. Among the names in his ledger is Yitzhak Maller, currently one of Natanya's richest inhabitants.

During the first five difficult years between 1927 and 1932 only six more Legionnaire families joined those of Sam and Avram. Already a number of the Legionnaires to whom Sam had sold shares in the Legion cooperative grove before he left the U.S. had given up the idea of settlement in Palestine and placed their shares on the market. Three of the Legionnaire families who joined Sam during those five years were American, the others were Legionnaire families who came to the cooperative from other parts of Israel.

The grove itself was an experimental orchard. To counter the dust and sandstorms which threatened the young trees, Sam devised effective windbreaks around the groves with castor plants. This was another Friedlander first which other planters were later to copy. Sandstorms were but one of the troubles; the Bedouin and hostile Arabs from as far as Tulkarm were another. It was then that the battle of the trees began, the enemy trying to uproot them, the Legionnaires their determined defenders. Sam well remembers the first five precious rifles issued to them by the Hagana*, the nights they lay in ambush until the raiding stopped.

There is something strikingly symbolic about this battle for the trees, the elemental fight between life and death with not merely a livelihood but a nation's rebirth at stake. It was for this the Legion had fought the Turks, this was why Sam Friedlander had returned.

Besides these, Lily had other problems. The Pardess could be defended, but her children could not grow up in a void. Where could they go to kindergarten and school? They had land in Natanya but they had not come to live in a town. Sam Friedlander, since the training camp in Nova Scotia, had held on tenaciously to his idea of a Legionnaire village. He would not go backwards from the Pardess Hagedud to a town. He could only go forward to the establishment of Avichail. The eight Legionnaire families at the Pardess were not enough to begin a pioneer settlement

* The defense force of the organized Jewish community before the establishment of the State of Israel.

but hope was maintained that others would join them.

When they started to come, it was without warning. Looking out of the window one night, Sam saw a light twinkling on a nearby hill. It was too low to be a star. No Bedouin would betray his presence in such a manner. Sam went out to investigate and to his complete surprise found a truck heaped high with building materials, barbed wire and two Legionnaire families. The joy of that reunion between three Legion soldiers on a moonlit hill could never be forgotten. Yosef Harussi had been in Sam's own company, and with him was Yosef Machovsky. They had fought and lived together. "We stopped with the last drop of wine." Soon after that happy night, more Legionnaires came with their families, first in ones and twos. Then, before long, forty families had gathered. These were the founders of Avichail.

Most of them were over forty years of age, half were of American origin. Both factors were to influence greatly the history and nature of their village, distinguishing it in many ways, even physically, from the usual run of cooperative villages already established in the country. Had they been younger men and women, in their teens or twenties, intensive truck farming would probably have developed as the basis of their village economy. Already, in the Pardess of the Legion, eight families had accumulated some experience of citriculture.

As a cooperative, Avichail started to develop extensive orchards and added to citrus such profitable tropical fruit as quinces, guavas and avocados. In the village grove each family had a holding of 2.5 acres, a further acre was allotted to each family to be used as it thought fit. Another was for the family home, its garden, trees and chicken coops. Gradually, Avichail acquired more land until its holdings totaled 800 acres, half of them citrus orchards, less than half for growing fodder crops, the remainder for the four-room family cottages, the streets and community buildings.

As mainly a fruit-growing village, Avichail has less of a farm look and more of the appearance of a garden suburb. Its closeness to Natanya certainly enhances this impression, especially as the outer streets of the resort town reach out to Avichail's first houses. One of them passes the original site of Pardess Hagedud which no longer exists as a Legionnaire grove but some years ago was sold to private owners. Near the site of the old Friedlander house stands a beautiful memorial building called "Beth Hagedudanim", "The House of the Legionnaires" — a gathering place for the soldiers of the Legion who are scattered throughout the country and the world. In the building are the records and trophies of the Gedud and the everlasting memorial of its fallen.

Avichail village counts today 140 families, four score of them the Legionnaire founders, some

their married children. All told, the population
has reached 600, of whom 430 are of membership age, the rest still at school. In fact, a third
generation is now growing up in the village, including the grandchildren of the Friedlanders.

Sam's house in Avichail, at the corner of two
streets, is always full of them. They, and the
village, are the Friendlander inheritance. They are
not, however, Sam's only claim to immortality.
Besides soldier, pioneer, immigrant, arms smug-
gler and founding father, another and unexpected
role adds still more to that rich complex that is
Sam Friedlander, the role of artist.

On a wall of the main living room of the Friedlander villa are three sun-splashed pictures, rust-
ic in theme, optimistic, strong — even exotic —
in color. They are scenes of village life, breathing
permanence, the mellowness of time. On another
wall is a beautiful original, a landscape, set in
Lithuania, by his father, Israel Friedlander.

Sam's studio, and most of his oils, are in a
chicken coop. His eighteen-hour day, which begins at five, now has more time for his painting;
it needs less for his fruit orchard. Recently, he
came back from a trip to Europe, "the first time
abroad in thirty years", he says. He returned with
fifty sketches and many more ideas from the
various countries he visited. When local artists
and publishers saw them they insisted on an album.
He is as professional as the best in the country,
and has exhibited successfully in both local and
national exhibitions.

Nevertheless, although he wields a brush as well as a spade or rifle, it is by the rifle that Sam Friedlander will be remembered. He just refuses to permit the Legionnaires' military tradition to be enveloped by the mists of legend and history. Nine years ago, when the Israel Army advanced into Sinai, Sam, at 69, was with them. No one could resist his demand to add his small pickup truck to the mechanized unit which reached El Arish.

"In the beginning, there was Sam." With him starts the story of modern American pioneer settlement in Israel. No other can claim with equal justice the title of its father. As for the mother, Lily Friedlander, or as both are called, Dror, her own words sum up this first chapter of its history: "If I had it to do over, I would still do it again."

CHAPTER III

Mendes Sacks — Citrus King

The large and juicy "Jaffa" orange still tops Israel's export list and its fame is wide-spread, particularly in West European markets. Every year millions of crates of oranges and grape-fruit pass through the gates of Haifa port and are loaded onto the swift and refrigerated fleet of the national "Zim" line. Most of this citrus is grown on the Coastal Plain where the sandy soil and sunny climate is so reminiscent of California.

Statistics show that some 400 Americans are engaged in private agriculture in Israel. Few Israelis, American-born or from other back-grounds, have played a more significant role in Israeli farming, particularly citriculture, than Mendes Sacks. He has shown that side-by-side with the kibbutz and moshav, the private farmer can also succeed on the land in Israel. As Mendes Sacks expressed it, "Agriculture is a business to-day. We all work together in it, the cooperative sector and the private sector. We're in it together."

A slim and dynamic American settler from

Baltimore, Maryland, Mendes Sacks is today responsible for the entire citrus operation in his
capacity as General Manager of Israel's Citrus
Marketing Board. Established by the Government, the Board supervises the country's groves,
the harvesting and packing of the fruit, technical
research, fertilizers and equipment, shipping and
exports. Mendes Sacks, the General Manager, was
appointed "king" of the citrus industry in the
summer of 1963.

It was no easy time to accept such a responsibility. Five successive years of drought had
affected Israel's citrus while in the following
1964 season rain and frost struck, damaging the
young groves in particular.

Mendes Sacks' history in the country began
in 1932, in the same year and on the same Sharon plain as that of Sam Friedlander's Legionnaire
village of Avichail. Sacks, however, did not come
to the Sharon region with any vision of establishing a rural cooperative group. He arrived as technical manager of a private company, the shares
of which were held by Americans and Canadians
overseas. "Gan Chaim", as the company was called,
held over 450 acres of citrus groves in the Sharon, near Kfar Saba and Raanana. Within a few
years, Sacks became full manager of the holdings
and built his home amid them.

It is not surprising that Sacks has been a successful citrus farmer since his arrival in Israel. Interviewed in January 1964 in his Tel Aviv office
headquarters at the Marketing Board, he acknowl-

edged the fact that he had been "born in agriculture". From an early age, he had never doubted that he would continue in his father's path. When he completed his studies at the Universities of Maryland and Harvard, he proceeded to specialize in citriculture at the University of California.

Mendes Sacks also married into agriculture, for his wife Celia, American-born like himself, is an agronomist. With her active cooperation at Gan Chaim they have experimented with various fruit in addition to citrus, like pineapples and avocados, and added other products such as artichokes and asparagus. Mendes is thus able today to leave his orchards and crops in the sure and knowledgeable hands of his wife.

In 1945 Mendes Sacks became the Manager of Pardess Syndicate, a cooperative of private citrus growers. He held this post until 1951 when he became the general manager of Mehadrin, a position he still holds.

Mehadrin has played an important role in Israel citriculture. Founded after the War of Liberation, when many groves had been destroyed and abandoned, when Israel was ingathering half a million refugees in two years and enduring severe austerity, Mehadrin was the government-sponsored program to establish new citrus groves on a sound financial basis.

Mehadrin took over abandoned and destroyed orchards and replanted them with trees. It has restored some 5,000 acres of orchards this way in various parts of the Coastal Plain, selling 3,500

acres of them, but retaining their management.
The buyers, from various parts of the world,
include Americans and Canadians. In addition to
the orchards, Mehadrin — under Sacks' steward-
ship — has acquired its own packing houses,
cold storage plant, water supply and a considerable amount of equipment.

Today, Mendes Sacks wears at least three
caps: he still manages his groves at Gan Chaim,
he continues to be general manager of Mehadrin,
and after years of membership on the Citrus
Marketing Board he is now serving as its general
manager as well. Mendes Sacks is also a Director
of Bank Leumi and of the Hebrew University. But
the Sackses continue to live, in Gan Chaim, in the
midst of their groves in the Sharon, on the soil
they love. Mendes Sacks' face wrinkles with smiles
as he describes his beloved home, its fruit and
flowers. And he is deeply proud of his Sabra sons,
the elder a lecturer at the Hebrew University,
the younger completing his Ph.D. in plant phys-
iology at Harvard University before returning
home to Israel.

It is thus more than clear that Mendes Sacks
is a man of unusual energy and ability. His replies
to questions are thoughtful and considered. In
the 32 years he has grown with the country's
citrus industry, Sacks has been constantly aware
of the similarity between conditions in California
and in Israel. Both employ similar methods in
their citrus cultivation, even though the fruit
varieties may differ.

Modern farming has always been large-scale farming and Mendes Sacks has always been engaged in large-scale citriculture, applying his experiences from California to the Sharon. Today Israel agriculture is highly mechanized, whereas in 1932 it depended primarily on cheap labor. The Citrus Marketing Board, founded in 1940, changed the nature of citriculture in Palestine, putting it on a proper business basis.

Another influence, according to Sacks, has been that of agronomists and soil scientists trained in the United States. Many of the country's best, he says, received their basic training at the Hebrew University and then followed this with an additional year or two at American universities. Moreover, agricultural literature and textbooks from the United States serve Israeli farmers as "vocational bibles". Above all, American farming itself acts as a constant example.

The year 1964 was the third in which Israel exported oranges to the U.S., in ever increasing quantities; it was the eighth year that citrus fruit was sent to Canada.

Mendes Sacks reminisced a little about other American private farmers in Israel. One of them, the late Nathan Fiat, who came here about the same time as Sacks, was a poultryman who became the headmaster of the famed Kaduri Agriculture School in Galilee until his death a few years ago.

Another friend of the Sacks family is Dr. Karmon (Weinstein), a horticulturist and citrus expert. Dr. Karmon ran the Department of Horticulture of the Agricultural Research Station in Rehovot for the Government for years.

Then there's Isaac Wineman who came from Vineland, New Jersey, some thirty years ago. One of Israel's leading poultry experts, Wineman still runs his chicken farm at Ramot Hashavim and serves as a breeding consultant.

There are many others, some in the last few years tending to gravitate towards research and teaching rather than towards farming itself. They keep on appearing in the news, usually associated with the introduction of some American method or an original innovation.

Another example of American agriculture settling in Israel, even though it came without a settler, is that of Sam Hamburg. As described in "Readers' Digest" several years ago, Sam came to Palestine in 1913. Then, after the first World War, in 1920, Sam Hamburg went to the States to study, and remained there pioneering cotton-growing in California's Central Valley and becoming a wealthy farmer. After Israel's independence, he became interested in growing cotton in Israel and it is due to his initiative and drive, as well as money, that cotton has become established as an important crop in Israel.

Although most American Jews are urban residents, it is estimated that there are about 80,000 Jewish farmers in the United States. Whether poultry breeders, citrus men or cotton

growers — some may be tempted to try their
hand at farming in Israel. If they do, they will
find that Mendes Sacks has provided an inspiring
example for he has demonstrated that Americans
can succeed in private farming in Israel as well
as in cooperative and collective enterprises.

CHAPTER IV

Youth Movement and Kibbutz Aliya

Avichail, in an historic sense, was the link between sporadic and uninterrupted American pioneer settlement in Israel. After it, most settlement assumed organized form. Those who subsequently established villages came from movements that could guarantee support and reinforcement from the United States and Canada. In Israel itself the new villages became affiliates of national village federations, enjoying their guidance, help, example and encouragement whilst the national settlement authorities provided them with the same aid as that given to any settlement, regardless of its members' country of origin.

Following the First World War a period of mobility began. Individuals left America for Palestine. New groups formed and disbanded in the United States. In 1924-5 efforts were made to start a training farm for would-be pioneers at Flagstown, New Jersey. During the summer of 1930 a group of twelve young men and women gathered for training at another New Jersey farm and in December of that year the "Detroit

Kvutza", as it was called, sailed for Palestine.*
Joseph Baratz, one of the founders of Degania,
then visiting America as an emissary of the
Palestine Jewish Federation of Labor, the Histadrut, had been the guiding spirit of this group.

The year 1930 was indeed a milestone in
American Zionist pioneer history. The first
trainees of the youth movement Hashomer Hatzair, which means "The Young Guard", left the
farm on which they had been studying agriculture at Earlton, New York. Their destination
was Mishmar Haemek, a Palestine collective farm
village that had been started in 1927. Their goal
was to obtain further training under local conditions as a first step towards starting their own
American pioneer settlement — also on collective lines.

The story of Ein Hashofet, for the Earlton
group were among the founders of this famous
Israel village, had its American beginning among
young Polish and Russian émigrés who arrived in
the United States and Canada during the twenties
of this century. It is in part related by Yosef
Wilfand, one of Ein Hashofet's founders, in a
booklet entitled "Ein Hashofet" (Palestine Pioneer Library No. 13, Zionist Organization Youth
Department, Jerusalem):

> "There were not many young people
> among American Jews of the twenties who

* A few members of this group are today in the
settlement of Ramat Yochanan.

were given to dreaming of Zion on this
Earth. One cannot even say that those who
termed themselves Zionists thought in terms
of actual participation in the upbuilding
of Zion. Even then, however, in the few
existing centers of the Hashomer Hatzair
movement, individuals made their appearance who had determined to go to Palestine from the States as a group. These individuals were scattered throughout the
country. Some were students at farm schools,
some were university students, and there
were some who sacrificed their personal
lives and devoted themselves entirely to
the movement. There were, as yet, no permanent connections, no planned guidance
emanating from Palestine. Hence laying the
foundations of Kibbutz Aliya Aleph rested
mainly on conjectures and the limited experience of the few who at one time had been
connected with Kibbutzim in the European
chalutz movement."

(Page 9)

Some words of explanation are necessary.
Terms such as Kibbutz Aliya, employed by
Wilfand above, may only be understood against
a background of the particular ideology and educational framework and methodology of this movement, Hashomer Hatzair. Before it, in the United
States, there had been only the organization Hechalutz, a broad framework for individuals seeking to settle in Palestine as pioneers. Small groups
of such individuals had been formed: in 1908
the group gathered by Eliezer Yoffe and more
recently the "Detroit Kvutza". Hashomer Hatzair,

however, became the first pioneer youth movement in the United States. It was not until 1935 that the second such movement in the U.S., Habonim, was established.

According to Hashomer Hatzair, a basic difference exists between youth organizations and youth movements. A youth organization may accept a body of principles or ideology and support them without requiring of its members that they fulfill such principles in their own daily lives. It may definitely encourage its individual members to fulfill such principles and live their ideology but will not make this a condition of membership. In contrast, the youth movement stresses that when its members are old enough to do so, they must live in accordance with the movement ideology if they wish to remain members. Otherwise, they are required to leave.*

Hechalutz formed in 1905, was in early years a pioneer Zionist organization. Some of its members fulfilled their ideology by setting sail for Palestine as pioneers, others did not. Later, it became a roof organization for the adult members of various affiliated groups who had committed themselves to such a pioneer life. The senior members of Hashomer Hatzair and of Habonim, committed as they were to pioneering, thus became

* They place pioneering at the center of their education. Adult members, that is above 18, who do not go to Israel are influenced to work on the local Jewish scene.

members of Hechalutz as individuals. This roof
organization either provided its own farms for
individual trainees or helped affiliated movements
establish their own on lines acceptable to it. Gordonia, which later merged with Habonim, was also
a fully pioneer youth movement in those formative days and an affiliate of Hechalutz.

The movements establish children's groups with
members from 10 years old and upwards because
their goal is not merely intellectual education, that
is the acceptance of certain principles and ideals,
but also character education, that is, training the
personality so that the individual has the ability
and will to fulfill these ideals. In this no difference exists between Hashomer Hatzair, Habonim
and the other youth movements.

Hence, the youth movement is a type of educational framework which tries to mould its members emotionally, intellectually and socially into
pioneers prepared for collective life in Israel by using scouting, and by providing, through its leaders,
personal example. Not all of its members, after
passing from age group to age group, fulfill its
ideals at the adult stage. It is, after all, a voluntary, spare-time association which has to compete
with the surrounding society, home, school and
street. In fact, the youth movement can be
likened to a pyramid, the broad base of which
consists of its large numbers of young children.
It tapers off as the children advance towards
maturity and are faced with the test of realizing
fully in their own lives the movement's ideals.

The culmination of this process, in the case of the Hashomer Hatzair youth movement, is the Kibbutz Aliya — the national organization of all members of adult age 18 and up dedicated to the ideal of establishing a collective pioneer village in Israel. This national unit begins its collective life before its members reach Israel by developing a community purse, training its groups together on a movement farm, establishing small communities living together in movement houses (whose residents often act as leaders of the younger scout groups) and by holding national gatherings, seminars and publishing its own journals. With an eye towards the needs of its future collective village in Israel, the Kibbutz Aliya influences its individual members towards vocational training most suitable for their pioneer life ahead.

Hashomer Hatzair in the twenties was the first pioneer Zionist youth movement of its kind to start working with American-born Jewish children, though there were Zionist youth groups of a non-pioneer type working by this time with children. It was the first to establish its own training farm in the United States; to assemble a Kibbutz Aliya (of 70 members by 1929) ; to send an integrated group of American pioneers to Palestine; and to establish there an American kibbutz, Ein Hashofet.

The background to this development is described by Yosef Wilfand:

"It was while these youngsters were thus dreaming and planning that the 1929 disturbances (in Palestine) shocked American Jewry out of its usual complacency and even aroused greater numbers of American Jewish youth to devote some of their thoughts to Palestine. Through the main thoroughfares of New York, Chicago, Detroit and other American cities, masses of American Jews marched in stirring protest demonstrations, and here and there one could see in these columns groups of young people who had made up their minds to throw up their studies and get on with this business of getting to Palestine. They were the adult members of Hashomer Hatzair who, in New York, for instance, had left their summer camp at Highland Mills to take part in the protest meetings. The same evening, after they had returned to camp, around the campfire, the idea of an American kibbutz was born... In the spring of 1931, the first group, composed mainly of Montrealers but including a number from the United States got to Palestine."

(Pages 11-12 ibid.)

Events in America during this period also influenced many young Jews. The year 1929, it will be remembered, saw the beginnings of the Great Depression, a development which shook the confidence of many that the United States was the sole land of opportunity. The depression produced sharp criticism of the capitalist system and the appeal of the socialist collective, the Palestine kibbutz, attracted some radical young Jews. The

democratic nature of kibbutz society, together
with its distinctively Jewish and Zionist function,
constituted for many a better inspiration than
did Soviet Russia or its apologists abroad.

Here, again, the youth movement contrasted
sharply with any adult or junior political organization. Acceptance of Zionism by its senior members meant living as Zionists, that is, leaving
families and homes in the United States and Canada and settling in distant Palestine. Acceptance
of Socialism meant living in a socialist way cre-
ating a framework of society which would permit
its individuals to enjoy a socialist relationship.
The starting point of the youth movement was
thus the individual himself, his capacity for self-
change and personal action. Through the individual, by voluntary endeavor, would the new society be created.

Ideology apart, the Hashomer Hatzair group
that set sail for Palestine in 1931 had nevertheless
much to learn. Although its members had had two
years of agricultural training and group life together before departure, they were still the very
first American group of its kind. Before its members was the very personal test of stamina and
endurance under extremely difficult and exacting conditions. They also were faced with the responsibility of having to succeed as the vanguard
of a new movement, watching expectantly and
hopefully thousands of miles away. Failure would
have challenged its existence, or at the very least,
seriously discouraged its membership.

The first graduates of American Hashomer
Hatzair were to be tested in another way at the
settled kibbutz of Mishmar Haemek. This little
village had been established by Russian and
Polish pioneers, members of a movement with, by
1931, a record of practical achievement behind it.
America, to the East Europeans, was not only a
land of opportunity but also, through its reputed-
ly high living standards, a place where affluence
produced "soft" and "spoiled" young people. That
any such "soft" Western youth, particularly the
sons and daughters of middle-class Jewish busi-
nessmen and professionals, could become Palestine
farmers was a thought that evoked the sharpest
scepticism and even laughter.

Thus the settlers of Mishmar Haemek did not
expect the first Americans to succeed. According
to Wilfand, "the stereotyped concept of the American settler, more like a fleet-footed tourist who
would soon retrace his footsteps, continued to
harry the first arrivals of this (American) kibbutz until they proved with their energy and per-
severance that stock phrases did not apply to
them. The period of training at Mishmar Haemek
was also one of consolidation and growth. At the
end of the summer of 1932 they left for Hadera
as an independent group". (Page 12, ibid.)

Their training at the veteran pioneer village
consisted of many things. It afforded an excellent opportunity of becoming familiar with a
typical kibbutz economy, based upon community
ownership of the land, machinery, livestock and

equipment, and worked by a central labor pool.
The trainees were employed in the farm branches,
and rotated among many of them to diversify their
experience; they also worked in the village service
branches, likewise all community-operated. In
short, the training received by the Americans not
only acclimatized them to work more than an
eight-hour day under a hot sun but also provided
the means of learning how a kibbutz exists as a
self-governing independent community. A group
of such trainees in a host kibbutz is usually referred to as a **garin**, that is "nucleus" or "kernel"
of a future collective.

Such nuclei (**garinim**, the plural form), in
those days, had to wait for land of their own
on which to settle permanently and build their
villages. It will be recalled that Palestine then
was governed by a British Mandatory Authority
and the Zionist movement, through its land pur-
chasing and reclamation agencies, had to buy
each additional piece of land, which usually consisted of uncultivated marshy or arid land owned by absentee Arab landlords. Each area occupied by a new **garin** advanced into the wilderness
the frontiers, both geographic and political, of
the State of Israel in the making.

Between the end of training in the veteran
pioneer village and the obtaining of land for its
permanent settlement, the **garin** spent its waiting
period in a condition known as **atzmaut**, literally meaning independence. That is to say, it occupied a temporary encampment and obtained its

collective livelihood from the work of its members as hired hands in the vicinity, usually in privately owned orange plantations and in various types of local industry. Hadera, where the Americans encamped on leaving Mishmar Haemek, provided facilities simultaneously for a number of such atzmaut groups.

Hashomer Hatzair, in the early thirties, had very definite ideas as to the requisite numerical and social strength of its pre-settlement groups. The ideal number, its members held, should be somewhere between 100 and 120 people. Moreover, such groups already in the country were expected to provide for the absorption of reserve forces that were yet to come from the movement abroad. The Americans had with their comrades of the first Kibbutz Aliya dreamed before departure of a kibbutz in Palestine entirely their own. Common background, traditions, culture and outlook — shared by all members — would in their opinion ensure a socially homogeneous and therefore successful kibbutz village.

Reinforcements from the United States did not arrive at Hadera as fast as the atzmaut group had originally anticipated.* In part, this was due to the difficulties of obtaining certificates of entry into Palestine from the Mandatory Government. At the same time, because the number

* Between 1931 and 1936 a total of 100 Americans came to the country and 40 of them left the group during the Hadera period.

of children in the American movement had grown, it became increasingly difficult to release senior members from their leadership and educational responsibilities. This meant delaying their departure for Palestine.

The group at Hadera, with excellent opportunities to establish itself on sound economic foundations if enlarged, had to give up its original ideal of an all-American kibbutz. It decided to seek a partner together with whom it would be strong enough to establish a new kibbutz. The consideration was by no means solely economic. Socially, it was dangerous for the collective to remain static in number. Not few such groups in the history of Palestine pioneering had disintegrated because of the social and cultural limitations imposed by restricted numbers. Rather than risk marking time until more members arrived from the United States, the Americans at Hadera began a search for a suitable union with a group of movement members from another country.

Whilst training at Mishmar Haemek, the Americans had made contact with a parallel **garin,** also in the parent village. Its members were the vanguard of a Kibbutz Aliya of the Polish Hashomer Hatzair that called itself "Banir". Rationing of immigration certificates for Palestine by the British had also prolonged the process of concentrating the Polish kibbutz members in Palestine. In fact many of them had been forced to wait year after year in Poland in their training farm at Czestochowa and, with the prospect

of further delay, had even returned to their youth
movement for renewed service as educators.

After the 1929 Palestine disturbances the Banir members, mostly from Volhynia in the east
of Poland, from Bialystok and Lomza, gathered
in readiness for departure from Europe and in
small groups joined others in running the British
blockade. The advance party reached Mishmar
Haemek at approximately the same time as the
first Americans and after completing its training
the Polish group also established an **atzmaut**
encampment in Hadera.

Banir also faced the problem of insufficient
numbers to establish its own settlement point. All
kinds of suggestions were made to them of mer-
gers with other Hashomer Hatzair groups. When
the idea was broached that Banir and the American vanguard should unite, both decided upon
negotiations which were to last a number of
weeks. The Americans had not yet fully given up
their purist idea of establishing an all-American
village and showing the country what Americans
could do on their own. In both groups misgivings
existed about whether the highly contrasting
backgrounds and traditions could produce an
organic union.

Here is Wilfand's description of their first
meeting:

> "It could hardly be termed successful,
> or enthusiastic. Bashfulness on either side
> was not lacking and the reticence about
> making any positive statements was great.

But the amalgamation was decided on, for,
if nothing else, both groups were blessed with
an abundance of horse sense (a quality still
attributed to Ein Hashofet even now, sometimes wryly, but never without appreciation),
and knew what was good for them. On the
eve of May 1, the Workers' Holiday, the
United Kibbutz sat down to partake of its
first communal repast together in the new
dining hall — and by then the mood was
indeed a festive one, for all sensed that a
new kibbutz had been born, one that was
destined to do great things..."

(Page 17 ibid.)

The America-Banir union had a joint
strength of 120 young men and women, sufficient
to establish a new kibbutz settlement point and
absorb further reinforcements from the United
States and Poland. We will return to it later.

Meanwhile, by 1932, important developments
had taken place in America amongst pioneer
groups other than Hashomer Hatzair. In that
year, through the efforts of various local Zionist bodies and the Histadrut in Palestine, a committee called Vaad Lemaan Hechalutz was
established by the following organizations: Poale
Zion-Zeire Zion, Pioneer Women, Farband, Avu-
ka, Young Judea, Gordonia, Young Poale Zion
Alliance, Junior Hadassah and the League for
Jewish Youth. All of these American organizations had taken a positive stand towards the concept of Palestine pioneering.

With the establishment of this roof organiza-

tion, a training farm for prospective pioneers
from all affiliated groups was started at Parke-
ville, Maryland, a journal called the "Hechalutz
Bulletin" was inaugurated and 14 branches of Hechalutz were formed with a total membership of
130. All of the 130 people from the affiliate organizations had decided to become pioneers in Palestine and were hence eligible to join Hechalutz
branches.

The development was by no means restricted
to New York. Almost simultaneously groups started in a number of other cities. In Minnesota,
for example, college students founded a training
farm of their own near Anoka. Twenty-eight graduates of Hechalutz received certificates that year
and left America for Degania Beth, a collective
village in the Jordan Valley. In December 1933 a
Hechalutz convention was held and the Vaad
Lemaan Hechalutz turned its affairs over to an
executive committee elected at the convention. Not
long after, another group left for Palestine. At
first they trained at Kinneret, and then proceeded
to the nearby kibbutz of Afikim. Members of these
groups were among those honored at the A.A.C.I.
Convention in 1963 when the Henrietta Szold
Awards were presented to Americans who have
been on the land in Israel for 25 years or more.

During the next years Hechalutz embarked
upon a greatly expanded training program for its
members and as a result a number of farms in
the East and Midwest and in Canada provided
facilities for agricultural instruction. The main

training center, however, remained in New Jersey
on the site of the Brown Farm at Hightstown,
leased in 1934. Two years later the Hechalutz
farm at Creamridge, also in New Jersey, was
purchased, and for more than a decade served
the pioneers of the youth movement, Habonim,
as a training center.

Because Hashomer Hatzair had developed the
kibbutz aliya idea, its immigrants left for Palestine with a definite kibbutz in view, which, of
course, was always one affiliated to the Hashomer
Hatzair federation of kibbutzim, Hakibbutz Ha-
artzi. Furthermore, other members of the same
kibbutz aliya came sooner or later to swell their
ranks. In the early days, the   non-Hashomer
Hatzair pioneers had no institution resembling
the kibbutz aliya, and could not therefore mobilize
a group large enough to set up a kibbutz of its
own, even in conjunction with partners. They
were free to choose their place of settlement from
among the many kibbutzim of the two Mapai (Palestine Labor Party) kibbutzim federations*, as well
as others.

For these reasons, only Hashomer Hatzair was
able, in the thirties, to establish "American"
villages. Long after the creation of Habonim,
that movement also evolved a framework for
ensuring   continuity   and   concentration   of
immigrants, which was called garin aliya, but
before that time members of Young Poale Zion

*Hever Hakvutzot and Hakibbutz Hameuchad.

CHAPTER V

"First Fruits"

In Palestine, the "temporary" Hadera encampment of Americans from Hashomer Hatzair lasted five years. At first alone, then with their Polish partners, the Americans waited for land to settle. It was given to them at the end of June 1937 and on July 4, anniversary of American independence, their advance party took possession. The site was Juara, a bleak and formidable height amid the Ephraim Hills. Around them were barren slopes seared by a pitiless sun. Below, the valleys could be made verdant again only after backbreaking drudgery in clearing them of their complement of rock.

On hills around Juara, men waited to add to nature's more than ample challenge. Upon the crests were the grey and forbidding houses of Arab villages. Armed bands used them as bases from which to attack Jewish settlements when the Arab assaults on Jews spread throughout the country from 1936 to 1939. In their very center, a dangerous hornet's nest indeed, Ein Hashofet began. It was a reavowal of life, an answer to death. The American settlement was but one of over thirty such outposts established in that year as a defiantly constructive answer to the Arab attacks.

A year after the American Polish village began, one of its founders, Shmuel Ben Zvi, added a page to Ein Hashofet's dramatic diary. Summing up this first twelve months, he made a striking comparison between this lonely pioneer outpost in the Ephraim Hills and that of the first group of Puritan colonists on New England soil. Between the groups was a time-span of some three hundred years, vast differences in conditions and objectives.

Yet...

> "Having wandered for many months over raging seas, they (the Puritans) finally reached the shores of a new, unsettled continent, only to encounter uncivilized Indians and fall prey to starvation and illness in the first winter. Yet at the end of the first year, they assembled to take stock and to offer thanksgiving for those that remained alive. That day was declared a day of celebration for themselves and for coming generations."

One hundred and thirty men and women settled Juara. Ben Zvi recalls:

> "...Soon, the old grey New England winter closed down upon them, and before summer came again, out of one hundred and odd persons, scarce a fifth remained. Yet all through those trying days in the shadow of death, they cut trees and built log

houses, and when the planting season arrived, they put out twenty acres of corn."

The settlers of Juara began in a summer as hot as the bleak New England winter was cold. They, too, walked in the shadow of death: Arabs struck some of their members down. They planted trees, built stone and concrete houses and when the season came, put out their acres of corn.

As for the "raging seas", Ben Zvi asks:

"And to what do one hundred and thirty people in our little world amount today in comparison with the masses of toiling people everywhere who are being ground to pieces between the wheels of life or tossed about by mighty waves on stormy seas? It is a number that pales into insignificance alongside the hundreds of bodies recovered daily from the bloodstained waters of the Yang-Tse, or compared with the thousands languishing in the concentration camps of fascist terror. Yet we have come, one hundred and thirty Jewish young men and women, sons and daughters of a beaten, persecuted race, we have come into these hilly wastes and hostile surroundings to build our home. We have come at a time when the entire world has been seized with a fit of madness."

Exactly a year before the settlers of Juara had "assembled to take stock and to offer thanksgiving", their advance party, a mere three score in number, left Hadera for Mishmar Haemek. They slept in the settled kibbutz one night, or to be more precise until 5 a.m. the following morning. At that hour, with the approaching

dawn, a watchman called them and they set out
for Juara. Mishmar Haemek, the village that had
trained them in their first year in the country,
fittingly launched them into the void of settlement.

Another American of Ein Hashofet, recorded
the event in the kibbutz diary:

> " 'All bound for Juara, awake!' Unlike
> other mornings, no time is lost in dressing.
> On this day of days, time counts. A hurried
> breakfast, and then we all rush to the open
> square before the library where the trucks
> are waiting, engines humming, ready to get
> going. The whole of Mishmar Haemek is
> awake, anxious to bid god-speed to the
> vanguard of America-Banir... Members of
> neighboring kibbutzim and even from those
> of Haifa Bay, have come to help us take
> possession of the site of the new settlement."

This is how Ein Hashofet began and in the
twelve months summed up so poignantly by Shmuel Ben Zvi in the leaves of its diary, they had
"come to know its every wadi and corner, its
every hill and cave. Our comrades have learned
to pick their way through ambuscades to fields
of wheat during nights of vigilant lying in wait
for the enemy on rocky hillsides. We have become
its citizens. Juara has entered into the life and
soul of every comrade, Juara with its hills and
ridges, with its vistas of myriad, motley, wild
plants and flowers".

Not only had the 130 men and women of the

settlement learned how to stand under fire and "to return it without betraying undue nervousness or excitement, to be calm and self-disciplined", but they had also learned to live as a collective. "Life as a Kibbutz," writes Ben Zvi, "puts one to an acid test. We knew that in times like these those who would fail us might be many. We also knew that those meeting the test would come out of it with renewed creative forces, typical of a period in which the old is destroyed, foundations laid, and a new structure erected."

Not many failed the group. In fact the record is astounding. It is the best of any pioneer village in the State of Israel. On the 25th anniversary of Ein Hashofet, celebrated at the kibbutz in 1962, of the 130 people who first settled Juara 105 were at the festivities. Of the remainder, 6 had died (some by enemy action), 5 were in other kibbutzim, and of the 14 who had left the kibbutz way of life, only 2 had returned to the United States. The others had settled permanently elsewhere in Israel.

* * *

The 25th Anniversary of Ein Hashofet was marked by one of the 1963 Henrietta Szold Awards being given to one of its founding members, to Shifra Geller, wife of Shmuel Ben Zvi. The Award presented by the Association of Americans and Canadians in Israel (Hitachdut Olei America Vecanada), is made to members who have distinguished themselves in particular fields of endeavor in Israel.* In 1963 the Association's National Executive decided that eight such Awards should be made to people "representing those who have been settled 25 years and more on the soil of Israel". Of course, Sam and Lily Friedlander were also among the recipients. Other recipients of the Henrietta Szold Awards in 1963 were Avraham Kaplan, a veteran citrus-grower who had come from Chicago in 1921, Nachman Ariel, a founder of moshav shitufi Beth Herut, Bertha Stav, one of the Americans who came to Degania Beth in 1933, Zvi Gutman from Minneapolis who has been in Kibbutz Afikim since 1934, Shulamit Beitan of Kibbutz Kfar Blum and Chaya Yerucham of Kibbutz Kfar Menachem.

These doughty veterans were honored both in their own right, and as a "minyan" of veteran American and Canadian settlers with long years on the land of Israel. The decision to honor these men and women as representatives of the Americans and Canadians in kibbutz and moshav was taken because 1963 was observed in Israel as the Shnat Harishonim (Year of the Forerunners) and marked the 25th anniversary of Ein Hashofet.

---

* At the presentation ceremony David Breslau, National Executive member, emphasized: "I am happy to report that we have in 94 kibbutzim a total membership of 789 adults... we have 239 members in 34 moshavim, we have 200 members in private settlements... together with their families, we have close to 5,000 people on Hityatshvut (pioneer settlement) in Israel today, former Americans and Canadians..."

In reviewing their first 25 years, the settlers of Ein Hashofet note that acculturation and group fusion between two so greatly different units as the Americans and Poles was no easy problem to handle, even for the most positive, courageous and successful members of both groups. If differences today are still discernible in Ein Hashofet, then they must certainly have been sharp and at times exacerbating and a source of keen friction, both in the Hadera days and during the first years of settlement. More important than the differences, however, were the factors militating towards coalescence, such as marriage and, above all, the exacting, creative task of kibbutz-building itself. Such a venture must necessarily absorb the devotion and energy of its collaborators, to the exclusion of personal interests. Those who were unable to sublimate their individual problems in the constructive totality soon left the kibbutz.

The Ben Zvis today make no effort to minimize or conceal the early internal frictions, the differences, and at times clashes of culture, and the residual contrasting characteristics of those who stayed and who are today the veterans of Ein Hashofet. "At the beginning both groups consciously elected central committees on a parity basis, later people were elected solely as individuals," he says.

Contrasting conditions of the United States and Poland being what they were, the Americans on the whole had come to Palestine with a higher level of professional and technical education. However, culture — in its broadest sense — is far from being limited to knowledge or vocational training. It pervades a thousand-and-one elements of human existence, the petty and the sublime.

So there were differences, small and large, even between two such groups dedicated mutually to the identical basic ideology, Zionist, Socialist, and collectivist. Few of the Poles, for example, knew Polish or liked Poland. Yiddish or Hebrew was their mother tongue. For both negative reasons (anti-semitism, cultural rejection and isolation) and positive (Jewish culture and pride, belief in Zionism and social justice) this was highly understandable. The Americans, on the other hand, knew English and liked their background. They had a favorable attitude toward the United States. In their daily lives, therefore, the Americans had a considerably greater advantage, both in inner stability and in the width of their intellectual horizons.

Perhaps this contrast, in itself, explains why two groups of Hashomer Hatzair, each infused with a fairly traditional Marxist point of view, should manifest such differences even towards political phenomena. The Poles, for instance, demonstrated a conservative attitude towards ideology and were more militant. The Americans were more prepared to listen to divergent, less orthodox and more varied opinions.

Besides variations of this type in the field of the "sublime", which must have often resulted in

clashes when concrete issues arose, there were
contrasts of a more modest variety. Already in
Hadera, when Americans and Poles worked in the
orange harvest, the additional height of the American girls must have been conspicuous. In the
kibbutz the American emphasis upon sanitation
and hygiene must at times have irritated the
Poles. The Banir people had been used to public
toilets in the farm communities in Poland. The
Americans insisted at Ein Hashofet on private
facilities attached to every family house and introduced a more expensive and certainly conve-
nient sewage system accordingly.

In fact the attitude of the Americans towards
personal comforts has been one of their distinctive
contributions to the character of Ein Hashofet.
It has been an attitude particularly apparent
among the American women of the collective.
They introduced widespread drinking of milk,
startled the Polish women members at first by
wearing red pants and the shortest of shorts.
Whilst the Poles maintained that "only the Go-
yim (non-Jews) eat tomatoes", the Americans
insisted that diet should include "lots of vegetables". The Poles, according to one American,
liked everything "either sweet or salty", the
Americans did not.

Though there were certainly differences which
were doubtless sharpened by youth and inexperi-
ence they were later blurred by increased maturity
and understanding, and the unifying factors far out-
weighed and outweigh them in the case of Ein

Hashofet. In fact, with mutual adjustment to the major demands of work, defense and collective living, such differences tend to enrich rather than impoverish the life of the kibbutz.

From the very first, this was discernible: "Well we remember the first months at Juara," writes Ben Zvi. "In a way, they were the 'honeymoon' of our undertaking. Notwithstanding the grave responsibilities this undertaking had imposed upon us, we were as though intoxicated at the first contact with the landscape, with the very wildness of the place. The first day, the arrival of the tractor, the first furrow, the new team of mules. And in this intimacy and buoyancy of the life of the small group, romantic legends began to be woven in midsummer night songs."

When men and women face creation and death together, in kibbutz and in marriage, the ties and traditions that bind them become stronger than those that divide them. There are no greater bonds than children and with these Ein Hashofet has been blessed in abundance. The oldest were 28 and 29 years in 1963. As of 1962 43 of the kibbutz sons and daughters had completed their army service. Another 40 were still in the ranks. Of the 339 members of the collective then, 86 were its kibbutz-born children who had attained membership age (18) and had been accepted into its adult community. Apart from these 86, there were another 195 children growing up and, in addition, 14 grandchildren. The first child had been born in 1934, the first grandchild in 1956.

As to creation of another kind, the wresting of a livelihood by pioneers from the barren soil, an insert from Ein Hashofet's early diary highlights the progress achieved between then and the present day: It is dated May 14, 1937, two months before the advance group occupied Juara:

> "I want to give you some impressions of our visit there. The farming area seems to lie to the south. We inspected about 250 acres and kept stumbling on stones all the time. The grain area is all under stones, though it looks pretty good. Mechanized labor won't be possible, at any rate not to begin with. These stones will have to be cleared off. Can't say anything about water. All we know is that boring a well is going to be an expensive proposition. The road to Mishmar Haemek is short but passes through non-Jewish land. The road to Yokneam is longer and paving it will take thousands of man days."

On July 24, 1937 a diary insert reads: "Today we began fixing up the spring of Ein Sus. It is in a very bad state of neglect, full of filth and refuse, and a great deal of work will have to be put into it before its water will be fit for use." The next day: "Our livestock is continuously growing. Adinah arrived today. She is a mare we have bought for patrol work and transport, from Kvutzat Hasharon, at the sum of L.P.22. At the same time, our dog had a litter of pups — eight of them!" On December 10, 1937: "We've just finished sowing the grain fields. There were

69.5 acres of wheat, 5 acres of barley and 21 acres of hay sown." December 21; "The flock is here. Sixty head, mostly ewes, and also five kids. This evening we sang in honor of the flock and Matityahu of Beth Alfa taught us shepherd songs."

These were the modest beginnings. On July 29, 1962 a report in the English-language daily "The Jerusalem Post", says this of Ein Hashofet's flourishing agriculture:

> "The veterans are glad now to hand over to the new generation. Ein Hasho-fet derives four-fifths of its I.L.3 mil-lion income ($1 million) from farming in almost all branches of agriculture, on some 7,000 dunams (1,750 acres) of fertile soil. Another 5,000 (1,250 acres) are fit for pastures only. Its only industrial venture, so far, is a flourishing screw plant 'Mav-reg', employing 25 people."

Of itself, Ein Hashofet, in its 25th anni-versary Hebrew publication, says its dairy con-tains 120 cows and 90 calves; for meat produc-tion there are 160 cows and 100 calves; its flock of sheep consists of 350 head; its poultry houses have 15,000 layers while meat production from the birds now stands at 400 tons per year. "Our sheep branch," according to the writer, "produces over 100,000 quarts of milk per year."

According to the same source the kibbutz now has 102.5 acres of fruit orchards (including apples, pears, plums, peaches and grapes); 112.5 acres of hillside on which are grown fodder crops for livestock as well as vegetables (carrots, cabbage and cucumbers) and gladiolas; 115 acres of cotton and sugar beet; and 1,500 acres of grass crops, all of them on hillsides.

Such minutiae may be of little value to the layman, but he is instantly impressed when he has the picture of the rock-strewn Juara site of 1937 before him. Every acre of soil had to be liberated from its burden of stone and boulder before planting could begin. The farmers of Ein Hashofet had not only to grow crops — they had to manufacture soil.

As to Ein Hashofet's life, the description "pulsating" does it little justice. It has a secondary school, serving four pioneer villages in its area. Its large theatre hall cum music center, seating capacity 1,200, houses music festivals and chamber concerts and plays by local and national companies to which the entire rural population of the area flocks. It has a permanent exhibition of antiquities found in its fields, including a unique collection of glass. Over 1,000 pupils have attended its Hebrew ulpan (six month intensive Hebrew courses for immigrants), most of them from English-speaking lands. In a special area is the new swimming pool and sports fields for residents as well as visitors. Around the kibbutz are the beautiful forests containing 6 million pines, forming the largest single forest in Israel.

A modest but impressive building has been

dedicated to the memory of members who have been killed or died. Their photographs and personal records are carefully kept here.

Ein Hashofet is a continuing memorial in its own right. The literal translation of its name is "The Spring of the Judge", and the Judge referred to is Louis Dembitz Brandeis, the very first Jew to reach the most eminent position of a Justice of the Supreme Court of the United States of America. Brandeis, influenced by the Puritan ideals of New England and the pioneering history of Kentucky where he grew to manhood, understood very well the meaning of America's first pioneer collective in Israel. When told by Shmuel Ben Zvi of the village's early tribulations, he once commented: "You are fortunate that you could have participated in such an enterprise."

CHAPTER VI

Kfar Menachem and Kfar Blum

Every five days, Fanya — a chicken farmer of Kfar Menachem — feeds 12,000 fertilized eggs into the incubators. Usually, they replace 10,000 yellow chicks and their debris of broken shells. Once again, she fills the empty tiers of wooden trays, adjusts temperatures and brings hatchery records up to date. This unceasing cycle, which by 1955 was producing 750,000 chickens per year, is one of the key operations of the largest egg-producing and broiler-processing farm in modern Israel.

The poultry industry of Kfar Menachem, although but a part of its mixed farm economy, is by far the most important profit-producing branch of the village. And, indeed, it fills a major role in bringing income into Kfar Menachem's community purse and is nourished by a number of other farm branches. For example, over 60% of the feed supplied to the birds — 550,000 broilers and 10,000 layers per year — grows on its own lands. Of some 3,000 acres of fertile brown soil, valley land cradled by the Judean

Hills, about 2,000 are employed to yield wheat, barley, sorghum and corn, all of which provide grain. This grain, together with imported fish-meal, oil cakes, meat scrap and antibiotics, com-poses the daily poultry diet.

On the remaining third of Kfar Menachem land grow fruit, vegetables and other crops. It has a sizable dairy, sheep pens, a carpentry workshop, garage and machine shops. But the first and lasting impression on entering the village gateway is of huge poultry houses that cover at least 12 acres of land, the broiler processing plant, the incubation center and, above all, the towering 500 ton grain silo, built in 1954 because the cap-acity of the smaller one nearby had been exceeded.

The story of Kfar Menachem's broiler industry begins with Aryeh Doron its director who came to Israel twenty-nine years ago from New York. A graduate of Rutgers Agricultural School at New Brunswick, New Jersey, he left the United States with American Hashomer Hatzair's second Kibbutz Aliya (Beth), twenty-four of whose mem-bers are up to the present day still in Kfar Mena-chem. That first group in 1935 consisted of 25 people. At that time, it will be recalled, the first U.S. kibbutz America-Banir was still in Hadera awaiting land for settlement. The vanguard of the second **kibbutz aliya** which started Kfar Menachem went to Kibbutz Ein Shemer for its year of pre-settlement training.

Unlike the Americans of Ein Hashofet, Ar-yeh Doron's group had to wait only two years

until actual settlement began on a permanent
site some 9 miles from the town of Gedera in
Southern Judea. In the same year as Ein Hashofet began at Juara on the hills of Ephraim, the
kibbutz of Kfar Menachem started its history as
a result of a combination of unusual circumstances. This second American kibbutz in fact
owed its auspicious beginning and its permanency
to the union of its members with a Polish kibbutz
group called Krit.

Krit started its immigration from Poland
as early as 1931 when its first members arrived
to participate in the Maccabia Sports Festival
in Palestine. It took the entire Polish group, all
told 70 in number, until 1939 to gather all of its
members in the country. By 1937, when the union
between the Americans and Poles was determined,
Krit had established an atzmaut point at
Hadar, in the Sharon, where it was running a
carpentry shop, producing furniture, doors, window frames and other items. But main places of
employment for the members were the nearby private farms and groves where they worked as
hired hands. With six years experience behind it
already, Krit as a collective group preparing
for settlement was by 1937 already high on the
countrywide list of pioneer units awaiting land.

As in the case of Ein Hashofet, when the outbreak of Arab riots on a large scale in 1937
prompted the Jewish settlement authorities to
reply by establishing new villages in the very
centers of the storm, Kfar Menachem was given

its land. Such new villages were placed on strategic heights, on sites dominating key highways
and in areas where Jewish settlement had not yet
penetrated. It was feared at the time that the
absence of Jewish settlement in a given area of
the country would result in that area being ultimately excluded from the Jewish State to be des-
ignated by the British Mandatory authority. The
Arab riots had in fact prompted the British to
dispatch to Palestine in 1936 a Commission   of
Inquiry which proposed   the partition of   the
country between Jews and Arabs.

Kfar Menachem was hence a "Tower and
Stockade" village. As its initial settlement group
occupied a site in the midst of a cluster of hostile
Arab villages, a technique common to all such
villages of the period was employed in taking
possession of its land. In the course of a single
day the settlers, with the aid of hundreds of
volunteer helpers, erected a defense point surrounded by a stockade and dominated by a high
watchtower from which a searchlight could signal
at night and illuminate the surrounding area,
probing for would-be attackers. Within the stockade, by nightfall of the first day, already stood
the first tents and prefabricated huts to accommodate men and equipment. The settlers, when
the volunteers withdrew, were standing in their
trenches rifles at the ready, awaiting the dawn
of a new day.

Gradually, as additional accommodation was
erected, the holding group absorbed reinforce-

ments. More solid houses, of concrete and stone, replaced the flimsy, uncomfortable and temporary structures. Stone-clearing and ploughing of fields started under armed guard, and around the encampment, defense points and the communications network between them were systematically developed. With the passing of time the Arab villagers in the area had to become reconciled to the fact that the new kibbutz was in their midst to stay. Only after attacks and unsuccessful attempts to destroy the new Jewish outpost, did the Arabs finally reach this conclusion.

There are few American villages in Israel that can with justice claim a tougher settlement history than Kfar Menachem. Not only had its hardy pioneers to face Arab attacks and severe isolation (in winter, particularly, its sole link with the outside world became mudbound and impassable when it rained); they had also to face dire economic conditions. There was no water, and there was the problem of age-long soil erosion. Much experiment was essential before the village land could be forced to yield crops. Of the 27 Americans who united with Krit to start the village, eight left the kibbutz in its first few years of history. Others from the second **kibbutz aliya** in America trickled over to reinforce the settlement group. In 1939 the kibbutz was further reinforced by a union with a group called El Gavish, composed of 50 members of the German youth movements Hashomer Hatzair and Werkeleute.

Aryeh Doron was one of Kfar Menachem's founders who fought out successfully the battle against man and nature. He was sent back to the United States by his village in 1945 to learn modern chicken farming. Realizing the physical limitations of its soil, Kfar Menachem had decided that a balanced budget would ultimately be achieved by development of a specialized farm branch not dependent on soil fertility alone.

In America, Doron made contact with Michael Peck of Lakehurst Farms, Lakewood, New Jersey, then one of the country's largest broiler raisers. Peck taught Doron broiler breeding and processing and by the time the latter returned to Kfar Menachem in 1949 Peck had also agreed to help finance the construction of the village's first building for the new project.

When Doron returned, with both means and knowledge to start Kfar Menachem's broiler plant, the then inexperienced Israel Ministry of Agriculture still opposed the project. "Bread and butter must precede meat," its officials stressed. Doron replied: "Instead of importing meat, we can produce it here." Without further discussion, the kibbutz began building its huge poultry houses and has never since looked back. What later changed the Government's mind, confirming the correctness of Doron's appraisal, was the Grant-in-Aid Mission of the United States (USOM), sent to Israel under the Point Four program. Its experts, invited by the Israel Government to begin operations, gave the kibbutz a sympathetic

hearing and as a result it obtained technical
assistance from both the Ministry and Mission.

Unlike the pattern of specialization developed
by the broiler industry in the United States, whereby separate farms, hatching centers and meat-processing plants have arisen, that of Kfar Menachem was of a combined operation. It developed
its own breeding flocks, began hatching its own
eggs, rearing its own broilers and building its
own meat-processing factory. About twenty-five
kibbutz members were soon employed by the industry and, together with Aryeh Doron, a second
New Yorker, Yehuda Ben Horin, became responsible for the operation. He, too, was sent to America to bring new poultry strains back to the
village and add them to the already predominant-
ly American varieties which had proven successful on the Israel market.

Since 1950, when Kfar Menachem's poultry
made history as being the first to be flown from
America to Israel, the stock has been essentially
white and grey Plymouth Rocks. According to
Ben Horin these "are excellent breeders" and
20,000 of them are accommodated in each of the
village's eight brooder houses. These are 300 feet
long and 40 wide and the birds are kept in them
until they are three months old when they are
transferred to the processing plant.

The plant itself, where poultry is killed at the
rate of 750 per day by a ritual slaughterer, is
otherwise fully mechanized. Feathers are all
plucked by machine and the chickens are packed

neatly in cellophane wrapping and cradled in flaked ice, produced incidentally by a machine bearing the nameplate "Carrier Corporation, New York". Output for home consumption, about two-thirds of a ton daily, is sent to the markets of Rehovot and Tel Aviv, the remainder is for export. According to Doron's calculations, it takes between 3.5 and 4 tons of feed to produce every ton of meat. The village has thus to supplement its home-produced grain with imports.

The organizers of Kfar Menachem's broiler industry maintain that its large-scale success is in no small measure due to the collective nature of the village. "The private chicken farmer in Israel," they say, "has not the resources for such extensive capital investment and expansion. The communal treasury of the kibbutz village, the combined profits of all the members, is far larger and more mobile." There is a great deal in the argument, for the kibbutz, with its varied economy, is able to switch profits from one branch to investment in another, and its community is prepared voluntarily to accept a frugal life in its early days in order to ensure prosperity for the next generation.

Kfar Menachem testifies to this fact. It started as a "Tower and Stockade" encampment on barren and waterless soil. Today, its land displays the lush green of grass and vegetable crops. A group of white cottage set among gardens and shaded by tropical trees has replaced the inhospitable, stone-littered settlement point, once surrounded by a barbed wire fence. Once again, during Israel's War of Independence, Kfar Menachem's settlers played an important military role. In July 1948 they captured the strategic height of Tel-as-Safi, an action which led to the occupation of eleven Arab villages in the area by the Israel Defense Army. The frontline thereafter moved far away from the village.

As to the name of the kibbutz, early in its history it chose Menachem Ussishkin, President of the World Jewish National Fund, as its inspiration — hence Kfar, i. e. village, of Menachem.

* * *

The members of American Hechalutz who left for Palestine in 1938 and 1939 went to such veteran pioneer villages as Ramat David and Afikim for training. Those who had been members of the American Young Poale Zion Alliance — Habonim, together with other individuals, decided in 1940 to join a kibbutz nucleus consisting of pioneers from England, South Africa and the Baltic countries which had concentrated as an **atzmaut** presettlement group at Binyamina.

This was a time of great difficulty for the **atzmaut** group. Unemployment at the village was rife. The Americans and their diverse partners sought and found work outside agriculture in stone quarries and in the Atlit salt mines, at building and other jobs, far from home. The private farmers of Binyamina and surroundings attempted to introduce cheap, unorganized labor

into their citrus groves and the local Workers'
Council of the area conducted a fierce struggle
against this in which members of the **atzmaut**
group participated. They were faced with both legal penalties and even physical assault. One member was "exiled" to Metulla for these activities.
An entry in the diary of the kibbutz dated Feb-
ruary 13, 1940 reads:

> "For the past three months we have been
> engaged directly in the struggle for Jewish
> labor in the moshava. This has meant stand-
> ing in picket lines day after day, clashing
> with the police, some of us landing up in
> prison. It was started by some 'Betarniks'
> (Zionist Revisionists — a right-wing youth
> organization) from Zichron Yaakov, who
> accepted a daily wage of 15 grush. It was
> only natural that this should lead to the
> employment of even cheaper Arab labor. We
> saw a group of 30 Arabs going to work pro-
> tected by a line of police and soldiers."

The next entry, dated ten days later, states:

> "The court trials continue. We are proud
> of the fact that there is hardly any one of
> our boys who hasn't been to court, some of
> them for interfering with Arab workers and
> others for 'attacking' a group of workers
> from Zichron. Ruth was summoned for
> striking a policeman... Have appealed to
> the High Commissioner against the fine of
> L.P.15. Ruth's trial is over. A week in jail
> or L.P.1 fine — each blow has cost us 25
> grush."

The "exile" to Metulla of one of the group was in fact one of the reasons why the entire kibbutz ultimately settled in Upper Galilee. Others joined the exiled member at Metulla and succeeded in establishing a number of new enterprises there. They began a rest home (one of the first to be under the auspices of a kibbutz), a workers' kitchen and a vegetable garden. Some worked for the Jewish National Fund surveying the marsh-ridden Huleh Valley; others for the government building program being carried out by the Histadrut contracting company, Solel-Boneh. A few acres of land for cultivation were obtained at Naame on a temporary basis.

Because of these first steps in the direction of Upper Galilee, the kibbutz at Binyamina decided finally upon permanent settlement there. The diary contains an item dated November 15, 1941 reflecting this:

> "We have reached our third year and our kibbutz is divided into three groups, Baltics, Americans and English. We are all united, however, in our aim to build a permanent home in Naame. Three years in the life of a kibbutz is not a long period. In the first year, the work position wasn't too bad. But in the second year, the influx of Arab labor into the orange groves compelled us to send out a group further afield. Our decision to send them to Naame was influenced by our desire to settle permanently in Galilee. Besides having earned our living what have we to show for our three years? A carpentry shop, a truck, a tractor, agri-

cultural implements, bungalows and farm
buildings, mules, a flock of sheep and a vegetable plot. We look forward to transferring
what remains here of our kibbutz to Galilee."

Thus stage by stage the kibbutz moved northwards, bringing with it all the movable property
it had earned by work. Last to move were the
mothers and first children, some the offspring
of recent marriages — English and Latvians,
English and Americans, or Americans and Latvians. Diary insert December 19, 1941 reads:
"Today we laid the foundation stone of our first
permanent house in Naame. The place was crowded with visitors, among them Berl Katznelson,
Harzfeld, Golda Myerson (now Meir, Foreign Minister of Israel), Berl Locker and others." The
others included the French Consul General, for
the kibbutz had decided to name itself Kfar Blum
after the famous French Prime Minister of the
time, Leon Blum, who was both a Jew and a
socialist.

The settlement site, 500 acres of land, through
which the River Jordan flowed southward, was
water-logged during winter. Connections with the
outside world were almost severed, the trucks
bogged down, mules sank in the mud, journeys
by foot were a miserable ordeal. Some of the
kibbutz members received training in carp-breeding at the nearby private fish farm of a settler
called Schwartz. Kfar Blum decided to turn the
experience to good use and transform its water-

logged land into fish ponds — a loss into profit. Water became a blessing in another way. The Jordan itself, running freely through the kibbutz fields, could be used for irrigation. Diary entries, of April 1945, record these developments:

> "We have just installed a water pump by the side of the Jordan. Now its abundant water can be exploited.
>
> "Part of our land is water-logged during winter and can therefore only be cultivated in summer. This area will be ideal for fish ponds and we are planning to start with 25 acres. The tractors have started excavating... Today the first fish pond was completed and fish, brought from Degania, have been put into it."

By mid-December 1945, Kfar Blum celebrated a great event. The road to the main Upper Galilee highway was completed and the village's produce could now be transported over it both in winter and summer: "No longer will we need mules, or have to trek through the mud. We are having a party to mark the event." The economy of the village by this time was based on the cultivation of every type of agricultural product, a clothespin factory, fishponds, the beginnings of a dairy and poultry branch. Future possibilities were bright as the village had rich black soil and unlimited water supplies.

Meanwhile, by 1946, post-war reinforcements had been arriving from England, Latvia, and America. The kibbutz now numbered 140 members, two score of whom were serving in the armed forces. One of them, Baruch Jacobson, was among twenty-two young Palestinian Jews who participated in a mission to demolish the Syrian pipelines in 1941. All were killed. An American died in Syria also while serving in one of the Jewish mechanized units of the British army.

By this time, too, Kfar Blum had seventy children, the oldest, few in number, of elementary school age. Their total was increased by the absorption of refugee children from Europe. Before long, the settlement built its first school.

Gradually, the face of Kfar Blum began to change. In place of tents and wooden huts, white concrete houses went up. In the midst of creation, however, came war again and destruction. The entry dated December 27, 1947 reads:

"The war has begun in the Jerusalem area and is spreading to Galilee. Until now we have suffered no direct attack. Are we prepared for the struggle ahead? Until now we have been affected only by the call-up and heavy guard duties."

Entry March 12, 1948:
"Today we received news of the death of Shaul, killed on the road to Hulata."

Entry March 19, 1948:
"Today Ari [Lashner] was killed by a bullet fired from Salchia, our neighboring Arab village."

Kfar Blum, as the first kibbutz of the

Habonim movements of America, England and
South Africa, from its inception was concerned
with the achievement of its second major aim
— to maintain contact with the youth of America, England, South Africa, India, Australia,
and New Zealand; it had become the focal point
in Palestine for the Habonim movements in these
countries. It built a world movement center, Beth
Habonim, on its land and there centered its
Contacts Office* (Lishkat Hakesher) formed
during World War II to keep members of the Habonim movement in the Diaspora acquainted with
its pulsating life. Kfar Blum thus served as the
training center for all types of Habonim study
groups including the Habonim workshop as well
as for the **garinim** prior to their permanent settlement. In particular, they had the hope that a
substantial number of Americans would soon
arrive to expand the community.

In 1962 Kfar Blum had 700 people of whom
260 were members, 40 of them born in the kibbutz. About 50 of the members were Americans,
eight born outside the United States. The total
number of children by that year stood at 300,
the remainder of the population consisted of
members' parents, and various training groups.

A description of the economy and population
of Kfar Blum, sixteen years after its history
began, is given by Shirley Lashner in "Arise and
Build", (Habonim publication, 1961) :

* Now Ihud Habonim, with an office in Tel Aviv.

"New branches have been added to round out our agricultural self-sufficiency: to the original grain and green-fodder crops, chickens, barn, vineyards, apple orchards and fish breeding, have been added beekeeping, cotton-growing, alfalfa, raising of chicks, pear culture, and seeded pasture land. Fish breeding and orchards remain our major income-producing branches... The combined income of our agricultural branches reaches over a million and half pounds annually...

"The personal service branches in which some forty percent of the membership works, include four distinct kitchens... the clothing stores for members and children... the mechanized laundry... a general store... sanitation... maintenance men for the children's houses... a medical staff consisting of a doctor, nurse, dentist, his assistant, a girl in charge of the hospital; and an office and book-keeping staff of several people.

"Our varied population of 700 members from the age of 18 to those who are approaching 50, plus temporary residents, candidates, children, and parents of members, all coming from over twenty different countries; people with family status ranging from single to families of four, five and six children; members who have been in Kfar Blum from birth (our Sabras), those who started with the first **garin** (nucleus) over twenty years ago, and those who just joined a year or two ago — assures a dynamic base to the community."

Since this description was written at the end of 1959 the economy and population of Kfar

Blum have retained the same essential characteristics. In 1962, work began on new buildings, including a permanent dining hall at last and a
large gymnasium, sport and meeting hall. Interviewed in 1962, one of the veteran Americans of
the group — looking back at the original relationship of Balts, British and Yanks — made
this comment : "At the beginning we (the Americans) felt closer to the Balts than to the
English because we came from a traditional Jewish background. As to the much-mentioned American know-how, neither we nor the British had
it. In fact we realized that both the U.S. and
English groups lacked ability, our experience was
theoretical, not practical. We therefore carried
at first but little weight in the affairs of the
community except when matters of general principle were being discussed. Nor did we shine in
organizational matters either. Only later, when
we gained experience, did we assume our right-
ful place in all fields of the kibbutz. What did set
us apart was a wider social consciousness, a
deeper faith in the ultimate, perhaps greater
tolerance, an inability to fall easily into line, a
capacity to try something new..."

Whether these views represent a general con-
sensus of all concerned or but those of a single
individual remains a question. What is certain is
that the original union was undoubtedly of three
greatly unequal parts, in number, tradition, cohesion and experience, with the Latvian group, initially, in a dominantly leading position. This man-

ifested itself in mastery of Hebrew and kibbutz management, although the Latvians, until the stage had passed, were patient, tolerant and went out of their way to create a feeling of equality. Had they not done so, the union would never have matured.

Nevertheless, it was perhaps this experience that decided Habonim's next youth movement generation to establish a strong **garin aliya,** the group which established Gesher Haziv. In the meantime, however, a new type of American village was founded.

CHAPTER VII

Moshav Shitufi

Avichail, it will be recalled, was not merely the first village of American pioneers in Palestine. From the day it started in 1932 it was also their first moshav. To many adult Labor Zionists, without youth movement background, but imbued with the concept of cooperative settlement in Palestine, the moshav was a more attractive ideal than the kibbutz. Most important to them, in comparing the two concepts of life, was the role of the family. Whatever the pluses or minuses of the kibbutz system, whereby children live and study, boarding school style, within a community of their own, it is most certainly less of a problem for graduates of a youth movement than for members of an adult Labor Zionist organization.

Although thousands of miles away, the discussion in America about the contrasting merits of the kibbutz and moshav systems of family life animated the ranks of the Labor Zionist movement. It was less violent in the youth movements Hashomer Hatzair and Habonim because both stressed the kibbutz pattern.

Within the various groupings of kibbutzim
in Palestine politically orientated towards Mapai
there was division of opinion and practice about
the education of children. Degania, for example,
the mother of the kibbutzim, did not believe that
at all ages children should sleep in separate accommodation from their parents, and for some years
they sleep in their parents' homes. Because the
early members of American Habonim, as individuals and in small groups, joined various kibbutzim in Palestine and did not concentrate in
one kibbutz of their own in the first years of
their movement, more than one influence made itself felt in the American movement.

For these, and other reasons, the Labor Zionist and Habonim movement is represented in
Israel by various types of kibbutzim and other
villages. Its first moshav shitufi — a settlement
combining kibbutz economy with moshav family
life — was Beth Herut. A second Habonim village of this type at a place called Kfar Lamm
on the Coastal Plain was established by South
African settlers. A signpost to it on the main
Tel Aviv-Haifa highway states simply Moshav
Habonim.

Beth Herut was not planned as a moshav shitufi, however. As an idea in the United States, it
began life as a moshav. The Labor Zionists who
first conceived it took their initial steps to establish a village in Palestine on lines highly reminiscent of those followed by the Legionnaires
who founded Avichail. These consisted of buying

individual plots of land on which their families
could ultimately settle in Palestine, from a Histadrut holding company, Yachin Chakal. The
company had sent its representatives to the
United States in 1932 after it had received land
from the Jewish National Fund and had undertaken to establish upon it three cooperative-type
villages, Herut Aleph, Beth and Gimel. The land
had been purchased from absentee Arab landlords and was suitable for citrus plantations.

In the United States and Canada a total of
59 families signed contracts with Yachin, all of
them members of the Labor Zionist movement.
Within the Yachin plan, they were to constitute
the farmers of Herut Beth. In 1933 a few of
the American families sent their children to Palestine to study agriculture thoroughly, under
local conditions, to ensure that settlement would
be successful from the moment their land was
ready for occupation.

Meanwhile, a conference of the 59 families was
convened at Chelsea, Michigan, to discuss the
character of their future village and it was here,
for the first time that a number of members proposed that the settlement should become a moshav shitufi, instead of an ordinary moshav.

Herut Aleph joined with other settlers at
Moshav Tsofit, near Kfar Saba and today 12
Americans live there. Herut Gimel (Herut "C")
never developed, Herut Beth (Herut "B") eventu-
ally changed its name to Beth Herut, (House of
Freedom).

There was complete unanimity about the moshav family system. All were in favor of the traditional way of life whereby children slept and
lived at home with their parents. The village, of
course, would be responsible for their education
and provide kindergarten and day school as elsewhere. The family, all maintained, was an independent and fully autonomous unit. It would
decide on how and what it ate, how its members
dressed, how its private budget would be employed. The majority at the conference, who de-
parted from the moshav idea, did so on economic
grounds. They advocated that instead of family
farms cooperating together through joint pur-
chasing and marketing of products and each
retaining its own profits or suffering its own losses, the kibbutz system of collective ownership
of the land and a common labor pool to work
it should be adopted. Profit, they said, would be
divided equitably among the families who would
spend it as they thought fit. In the kibbutz profit is divided equitably and distributed as goods,
each item of budget being decided by the general
meeting or a committee.   A minority of participants, from the Eastern seaboard, rejected the
"moshav shitufi" idea.

Following the Chelsea Conference, that decided
Yachin should deal directly with each individual
family, offices were established in New York and
in Minneapolis. A second conference at Cleveland
twelve months later adopted the moshav shitufi
practice as already evolved by villages of this

type in Palestine. Instead of standard type
family housing usually provided by the
village as a whole, Herut Beth was to have
houses built by each of its families according to
their own individual taste and budget. Secondly,
each family would have a little more than a half
acre of land of its own around its home and it
would work this land as it wished and for its own
direct profit. In Cleveland the group assumed
collective responsibility for financial commitments
and obligations to Yachin as some of its members
found, due to the depression in the United States,
it was difficult to meet them. By this time the
number of its participants stood at 60.

As the contract with Yachin was about to ex-
pire in 1936, a new agreement was signed with it
by the group whereby the company would continue preparatory work on the young orange
groves. Three years later a few of the older members of Herut Beth, together with the youngsters
who had graduated from Mikve Israel Agricultural School, assumed responsibility for the American families as they moved across the Atlantic
and Mediterranean. They registered the cooperative with the British authorities as a legal
entity and the name of Herut Beth replaced that
of Yachin. With everything ready for the complete settlement of the American group, war broke
out and delayed the immigration of many of its
members.

Among the first families to have settled on
the land by 1939 was that of Aryeh Messerman

of Boston who started building his home as early
as 1933. Then came Isaac and Sonya Foreman
of Kansas City and Nachman and Sybil Ariel of
Chicago and New York, respectively. Sybil's
father, incidentally, an organizer working full
time for the Labor Zionist movement in America,
had been one of the initiators of the entire group
project. These first families had no children and
they derived their income from working as hired
hands for Yachin whilst the company was ful-
filling its contract to prepare the land. The others,
who had children, were advised to wait in America until the land was profitable. Hence, besides
those mentioned, only a few more families arrived
before war broke out.

Meanwhile, in the United States, Young Poale
Zion-Habonim was still a small movement. When
their idea of a moshav shitufi was made known
by those waiting to leave for Beth Herut, there
was a shocked reaction from some members.
It is of interest that among those who then expressed condemnation at this deviation from the
kibbutz principle were a number who settled in
Kfar Blum and eventually left that kibbutz to
become members of Herut Beth.

During the war years, when a total of ten
families had gathered at the Herut site, the remaining members of the moshav shitufi in America helped the settlers. There was no market in
Palestine for the first fruit of the groves and it
was buried in the ground. Three of the families
left and returned to America, but one of these

later reconsidered and returned to Israel. When the war ended, the other families started to come over, at first in a trickle from 1946 to 1948 and then in larger numbers. By 1949 a total of 49 families had arrived. Of the others still in America, some had children in Kfar Blum. When their children decided to leave the kibbutz they claimed their **chelkot** at Beth Herut and became its members. There were 15 such ex-kibbutz families. The plots that remained were purchased for members of the original group in America who in the meantime had decided to remain there.

Herut Beth's limitation that only 60 families could share its economy and compose its population produced its own crop of problems. It is true these are not unique for they face other moshavim shitufiim and moshav type villages. Most revolve around the fate and future of the village children when they reach the age of maturity. When the first son of a family reaches 21 and marries, his father can make him a partner to his share and offer him building space for a home on his more than half acre of land around the family house. The son is hence entitled to all the same rights and privileges as the other full members of the village community.

When there are two or more sons in the moshav shitufi family, the village economy can offer them no solution. They have to seek settlement elsewhere in either village or town. Of the shares held by members of Beth Herut by 1962, four were already partnerships of father and son. There were three or four full shares for sale to potential members under 35 years old who had two-thirds of the cash value available for downpayment. In the summer of 1962, the value of each share was I.L.10,000. To the purchasser this provided a plot of 2.5 dunams (4 dunams = 1 acre) on which to build a house at his own expense, the right to work in and draw family income from the economy as all other members, and equal ownership in the village.

The income, or "salary", drawn in 1962 by each Beth Herut family varied according to the number of its souls. A couple with three children, for example, would receive monthly I.L.330; with two children I.L.315; and without children I.L.290-300. These totals, however, do not represent the full picture. From time to time dividends are paid out when profits are high. In addition to this direct income, the village treasury pays all taxes and for education, health and other services. Apart from this, each family's income is further augmented by the proceeds of its plot of land or meshek ezer, as it is called.

Most members of the village grow on this plot sufficient fruit and vegetables to meet year-round family needs and keep a controlled (by general assembly decision) number of chickens and turkeys. The 1962 limit stood at 400 laying hens and 600 turkeys per family per year for which the village provided the feed. Through its cooperatives each family's surplus eggs are marketed. The price fetched, minus the cost of supplied feed,

provided each family with its profit, estimated
annually in 1962 at somewhere between I.L.2,000
and I.L.3,000.

The family salary, graded according to the
number of children, but otherwise equal, is drawn
of course from profit made by Beth Herut's cooperative economy. The remainder of this profit
is ploughed back into the branches, village property and livestock and equipment. The economy
itself is based upon a total communal land holding of 525 acres, one of the largest turkey farms
in Israel, and an extremely successful silk-screen
printing plant. The farm branches consisted in
1962 of: 250 acres of citrus groves; 87.5 acres
of fishponds; 37.5 acres of bananas, 37.5 acres
of quinces, guavas and other fruit trees; and 50
acres on which family housing and the 2.5 du-
nam family plots are sited. Serving the farm are
2 trucks, 8 tractors, a garage, metal and carpentry workshops.

Shohar Studios as the Beth Herut screen-
process printing plant is called, has become nationally famous. It reproduces on all sorts of
materials advertising display, art work, photo-
graphic reproductions, and prints designs on plastic
tablecloths, shower curtains and nylon bags. Shohar in 1960-61 did a total business of more
than I.L.350,000. The plant was started in 1950
by two members of the village, Carl Allentuck
and Lionel Bassis, both of whom had many years
of experience in color printing in the United
States. It employs 30 people, including 11 mem-

bers of Beth Herut, and as just one of its projects, daily prints designs using up to seven colors on over 3,250 feet of plastic materials.

Work in Beth Herut consisting of an eight-hour day is organized as in a kibbutz, with one important difference. Whilst its menfolk constitute a common labor pool, and are employed daily in the various farm branches and at the printing plant according to need and skills, the women of the village are not required to work. If they do so, and some are employed, for example by the printing shop, they are paid full salary rates like outside hands. Otherwise, they combine domestic duties with looking after the chickens and turkeys on the family plot.

Although Beth Herut pays for the education of all its children from 3 years old until the end of high school, it has only a small kindergarten on its site. Children of the first eight grades attend school at nearby Kfar Vitkin, a moshav, whilst most of high school age are enrolled in the regional school of Kfar Monash. Others of this age attend various trade schools. University education is still a family decision and its cost, a family responsibility. Several young people of the village are at present studying abroad. In 1962, there were 200 children in Beth Herut.

Each year, at a meeting of its general assembly of 116 members, Beth Herut elects its governing executive. This election follows detailed reports given by the outgoing executive and various committees. In addition to the executive, composed of a secretariat of 3, plus 4 other members, the village elects its Financial, Planning, Meshek Ezer, Youth, Cultural, Education, Women's and Control Committees. The general meeting, supreme body of the community, meets each two to three weeks and decides on principles and policy. The executive and committees carry out policy in their day-to-day activities.

Central institutions of Beth Herut are its large cooperative supermarket-like general store, the **tsorchaniya,** which is run strictly on a commercial basis by the village (it sells its wares to village members and outsiders at the same price and makes no profit but merely covers overhead and salaries), and the Beth Am. The latter, built in 1958 at a cost of I.L.123,000 consists of a large, modern assembly hall, complete with stage, which is used for general meetings and festivities.

The standard of living is generally acknowledged by both inhabitants and associates of Beth Herut as being among the most advanced of the villages of the same age in the country. Its living standard is actually higher than that of many an older settlement. This is obvious from a first glance at the average housing unit, consisting generally of a four- or five-room cottage, with beautiful gardens, lawns, trees and general landscaping. Beth Herut, just off the main Tel Aviv-Haifa coastal highway, has no reason to complain of isolation. Nine miles to the south is the attractive seaside resort of Natanya, next door are Kfar Vitkin and beautiful beaches.

Within the village, the population today consists of 60% Americans and Canadians, (plus a few English and South Africans who strayed into membership), whilst the remaining 40% are made up of Sabras as well as Russians, Latvians and other Europeans. There are a half dozen other families living on the site who, although not share-holding members, were given plots on which to build their homes as they are permanently employed by the village. They include a teacher, architect and dentist.

A veteran American at Beth Herut has noted: "The Americans have stamped their distinct imprint upon this village in a number of ways. For example, Beth Herut's prosperous look, its housing standards, its lawns and landscaping are all due to our direct influence. There was resistance towards spending so much on landscaping on the grounds that it was unnecessary luxury. Now that it exists, everyone is pleased. The general lines of cooperativism, how we worked out the moshav shitufi idea, also stems originally from the American group. They and their children were the bearers of the idea and carried it out, the others accepted and followed."

Family life in the moshav shitufi, as in the moshav, is certainly most stable. In Beth Herut, for example, out of its 60 families there have been only three cases of divorce. On the other hand it is not the type of village that is possible for unmarried people. A bachelor or spinster cannot live in a moshav shitufi amid established families. Social life in 1962 was described by a member: "For those who want it, we attempt to give intensive activity. We have plays and movies here and bring artists. This is not too difficult as Natanya and Tel Aviv are not far away. We have study groups on various subjects and a choir, although the latter is not at present functioning... Sports are mostly for the kids... we are getting too old and tired (average age of village founders now 40). We have a good Hebrew library."

In answer to a question about attitudes towards religion, a fairly representative reply from an American founder was: "The majority don't light candles on Friday night but on the High Holidays, Rosh Hashana and Yom Kippur, they attend synagogue. Whilst the Sabras are definitely anti-religious, the American group, particularly those from Minneapolis, had a sound Jewish education and are traditionalists."

And that was Beth Herut, a thriving American village of the moshav shitufi type on the Coastal Plain, in the summer of 1962.

CHAPTER VIII

Hatzor — Youth Movement Kibbutz

The Second World War interrupted the flow of American pioneers to Israel. Graduates of the various youth movements were called up to the army, navy and merchant marine as soon as they reached combat age. Training farms, established in the United States as miniature collectives, were maintained with difficulty. Groups sent to them shrank in size and consisted mainly of young women. In the cities work among younger age groups became more difficult as there was a dire shortage of youth leaders. Those who remained in America faced new problems as educators and as graduates ready for **aliya.**

Under these conditions, the third Kibbutz Aliya (Gimel) of American Hashomer Hatzair had a challenge to meet. It responded magnificently. Throughout the years of fighting, its members maintained contact with each other under the most trying circumstances. Those in the armed forces sent into the **kibbutz aliya's** treasury a part of their pay, the others their entire salaries, minus amounts essential for living expenses based on a

standard set after general discussion. Members
continued to lead younger groups despite the
fact that they were getting too old for such tasks.
Vocational training for the future kibbutz in Palestine was carefully planned. It consisted not only
of periods on the movement's training farm but
also more specialized preparation which would lead
to the establishment ultimately of auxiliary economic branches.

The loss of six million Jews, a third of an
entire people, can never really be recouped. The
Jews of Poland and Russia, for instance, were the
heart of world Jewry, the center of Jewish renaissance in the 19th and 20th centuries. From
them sprang the two greatest Jewries that survived the war — those of America and Israel. In
Polish Jewry had reposed the most profound national riches of history, memory and culture. From
the Jewish communities of Poland, small or large,
had emerged the creative energies of Jewish sur-
vival, the movement to re-establish national sovereignty upon an ancestral homeland. The **chalutz**
movement, in all its forms, had been the fountain-
head of this national will to survive and rebuild.

When the war ended and a horrifying pall of
smoke and ash was all that remained of millions
of Jews, three very small reserve forces
of trained people were all the pioneer settlement
movement in Palestine could look to. The first
were the survivors of Europe, the handful of individuals who had been members of great movements, and the orphaned adolescents rescued by

the Youth Aliya organization that trained them
as settlement groups. The second source was the
small pioneer movement of Palestine itself, the sons
and daughters, locally-born or educated, of veteran pioneers. The third was the small **chalutz**
movement, struggling against the stream, in the
Western world.

Hatzor, as a kibbutz, was to become a com-
pound of all three categories. The Americans of
Kibbutz Aliya Gimel were to unite in Palestine
with a group of Bulgarian and local youngsters
who had already established a pre-settlement
point in Rishon-Le-Zion. The first of the Americans to arrive in the country joined them in 1945.
In their earliest years together this union of
graduates from the American and Palestinian
movements of Hashomer Hatzair (for the Bulgarians had also been educated by the Palestine
movement) became known as "the puritan kibbutz". Although Hatzor's members today look
back at the description either with a smile or a
degree of resentment, they admit it was then
merited, at least in part.

Both Americans and Palestinians had similar
objective reasons for being extremists in form. All
of them, militant Jews and socialists in ideology,
had by history been denied the opportunity of
saving any of the six million Jews incinerated
in Europe. They had been witness to the slaughter
with a feeling of impotence and despair. Those
that had fought in the armies of the United
Nations had done so under foreign flags. The

war's end must have found in both groups a mighty determination to implement their ideals.

There is another factor, common to Western youth and Sabras, that tends to produce maximalism in their youth movements. Neither are forced to uproot themselves from their countries of origin. The Americans, for example, do so solely from choice. Needless to say, it requires strong idealism and character to leave families they love, a culture which is their own, a standard of living that is high, to become peasants in a distant barren land, to learn a new language, to become part of an entirely different mode of existence. The movement is hence a filter through which only the strongest and best prepared pass on their way to pioneer settlement in the distant homeland.

The Sabras, on the other hand, are already in the national home, from birth. They need no Zionist ideology to uproot them from one country in order to settle in another. Their patriotism towards Zion is as natural as that of an Englishman to his country of birth. The revolutionary expression of the pioneer Sabra hence tends to concentrate in two aspects of the **chalutz** ideology. The first is the pioneer role he assumes in leaving Tel Aviv or Haifa for the parts of his country still wilderness. The second is the change in spirit needed to fulfill this new role. The common denominator of the American and Sabra pioneer is thus change of character, of behavior pattern. It reasserts itself almost in direct ratio to the absence of those political and social pressures once constantly present in the case of the East European **chalutz.**

Hatzor, in this light, from its earliest days was a marked contrast with the villages of Ein Hashofet and Kfar Menachem which preceded it. Experience of kibbutz life has since progressively narrowed these differences but at the beginning they were singularly apparent. Coming from militant youth movements, situated geographically in free democratic societies, the American and Israeli partners of Hatzor began building their kibbutz along lines which were a reversion to the earliest days of the kibbutz movement in Palestine, the days of its adolescence. There are two striking examples of this. The first is how Hatzor organized its "communa" in its initial years; the second was its attitude to smoking.

The early type of communal wardrobe in the first kibbutz type villages was that known as **machsan aleph.** All clothing, heavy or light, was kept in a common store and distributed each week. The concept of private ownership of an article of clothing was unknown. In time, almost every kibbutz changed to **machsan beth,** a system under which every member was issued equal amounts of clothing which bore his initials or an identifying number.

Despite the fact that almost every kibbutz in the country by 1945 was employing the system of **machsan beth,** Kibbutz Hatzor resolved when it was founded to reintroduce that of **machsan**

aleph. No one could receive private presents from his family in America or Tel Aviv. Radios were rotated or programs fed to family rooms where speakers were installed. This rigid system of collectivization of all personal property remained for some years.

As was the case with **machsan aleph,** the smoking ban could not be indefinitely maintained. Common sense and maturity prevailed. Both examples, however, were symptomatic of the puritan atmosphere of the early kibbutz. As a measure of their maturity today, members look back on these examples with embarrassment. Philosophically, however, there is one justification in the light of Israel's overall experience since. It is the maxim that: "The secret of living is to retreat as slowly as possible from original ideals." Better to begin with the maximum than to compromise further from a middle position.

A sign, perhaps, of the changed atmosphere of Hatzor was the gradual appearance of cosmetics, something once regarded with abhorrence by members of the youth movement. Bella — one of the kibbutz members — was sent on a course in 1962 to learn hairdressing and cosmetology.

Many other changes have overtaken Hatzor since first it became a united group at Rishon-Le-Zion during its pre-settlement stage. The union then, of 69 Americans and some 70 Sabras and Bulgarians educated in the country, was not free of initial difficulties. It took the Americans almost

five years before they could share in the administration of the kibbutz, that is until their
Hebrew became fluent enough to either handle
outside relations or chair meetings of the general
meeting. Compared to their partners', their training was far from adequate for conditions specific
to the country. Their average age was 27, well
above that usual in settlement groups. Some were
married and arrived at Rishon with children.

Exactly 38 of the first 69 Americans remained,
despite all of the initial difficulties, including the
hard living of the first years, inter-group frictions and tensions and war. Of the 22 who left,
and not a few did so because of the puritan
stand of the group in its earliest years, only 6
returned to the United States. The others (in the
main), settled in such development towns as Beersheba, few in such large urban centers as Tel-
Aviv, Haifa or Jerusalem.

Like other such groups, Hatzor laid the foundation of its economy while still in the **atzmaut**
stage at Rishon-Le-Zion. During that initial period,
it worked a piece of land, saved the earnings of
its members who were employed in the local
orange groves and vineyards, and began the machine shop which today is the sizable factory
producing irrigation and electrical equipment called "Omen Metal Products". It also experimented
with an electronics enterprise in its first few years
but this, because of marketing difficulties at the
time, did not succeed. Another project of the
early kibbutz was its mechanized carpentry shop.

The Americans of Kibbutz Aliya Gimel brought
with them to Hatzor much of the initial machinery and equipment for all these projects for which
they had saved throughout the Second World War
years.

The land the kibbutz occupied in 1947 consisted of 1,500 acres all told. Within 15 years the
farm economy had developed to the point that its
annual turnover totaled $900,000. Branches in
1962 consisted of: 750 acres of irrigated crops,
including cotton, vegetables, beets and deciduous
fruit; 150 acres of citrus plantations; 12.5 acres
of vineyards; 12.5 acres of bananas; and the remainder grass crops. In addition, the farm economy included poultry (10,000 birds) and cattle
for beef raising (200 head). By this time, the
castings factory had become a serious enterprise,
employing 50 people and was at the beginning
of a $250,000 expansion program.

"Omen Metal Products" had developed by
1962 four principal departments: 1) Irrigation
equipment such as aluminum couplings, fittings,
and valves for portable irrigation systems;
2) Sanitary fittings like stopcocks, bibcocks and
gate valves; 3) Metal-clad electrical fittings, such
as switches, junction boxes, reducers, inspection
elbows and fuse boxes; 4) Die-casting contract
jobbing. This section produces castings for other
factories, making, e. g., low pressure gas regulators
and valves, water meters, electric watt meters
and electric motors. The factory is an independent
exporter and its products have been shipped to

Turkey, South Africa, Burma, Italy, Kenya, Ghana, the Philippines and other countries, winning an excellent reputation not only because of their quality but also because of their lower prices in the face of American and British competition.

Pride of "Omen" is its Vacumatic Casting Machine invented by David Morgenstern of the United States, which represented an investment of $40,000. It eliminates any possibility of air bubbles forming in castings. With its expansion program, to be completed by 1965, the enterprise expects to employ another 50 workers and increase its output not only of aluminum and zinc products but also of various brass castings. At present, the first two departments of the factory alone have an annual turnover of $130,000. One of the advantages of the enterprise for Hatzor will be its capacity to absorb the labor of the community's second generation, a problem facing many such villages because of the economic limitations of their farming branches.

It is in this second generation of Hatzor that the differences between the original groups are scarcely discernible. Perhaps the only distinguishing feature suggesting whether parents are Americans or others is the standard of English in the classroom. Hatzor, among its total population of 500 by 1962, counted 220 children up to 18 years of age, 10 who had completed their army service and returned as full village members, and another 23 who are still in the army and will join the village on demobilization. Its membership, including the ten Hatzor-born members, numbers 200. Parents of original members and training groups make up the remainder. A breakdown of the 190 senior members in 1962 produced the following table of origin: Americans 38, Sabras 42, Bulgarians 25, Poles 10, Germans 10, English 6, South Africans 4, others 55. The others included people from China, India, France and various countries of North Africa and the Middle East.

The village itself, now 15 years old, has reached in appearance the stage midway between camp and park. The most developed area has its lawns, flower gardens and beautiful shade trees. Pathways are of inlaid stone. The dining hall is still not permanent, although it is the best of the prefabricated kind in use by kibbutz villages. Large, wide and airy, its tables seat four people, a great improvement over the earliest kind around which 6 and 8 people sat in congestion and discomfort. Most of the village veterans are housed in one-and-a-half-room family apartments. The latest, now being built, are dubbed "cottages" according to Israeli custom. These are 2-roomed, split-level units, the sleeping area above the living room joined to it by a stairway. Like many kibbutz villages today, Hatzor has joined the "swimming-pool club". This virtual epidemic of brand new swimming pools has been financed by German restitution payments to members who suffered losses at the hands of the Nazi regime and all of whom have turned their money over to the kibbutz treasurer.

As to life in the village apart from work,
everyone emphasizes that it is richly cultural.
The claim is supported by the network of study
and other groups, constantly at work in the
evening hours. Hatzor takes pride in its flourishing choir and a no less active dramatic circle.
The latter puts on two or three plays per year.
Study groups include mathematics, Bible, literature and a variety of other themes. As to social
trends, Hatzor boasts of a developing "matriar-
chalism" for which no one dares to blame either
the original Americans or the Sabras. The fact
is that in 1962 the village secretary, treasurer
and two members of the committee that allocates
work were women. As to politics, despite the apparent monolithism of the Mapam line, members
of Hatzor claim a highly critical approach to
Russia "since the 20th Congress of the Communist Party of that country when Khrushchev made
his famous speech, indicting Stalin." This reserva-
tion is held jointly by Sabras and Americans.

In the village tradition, a proud place is given
to the heroic stand of its members during the
Israel War of Independence. Hatzor then stood
in the path of Egyptian armored units making
a major thrust northwards towards Tel Aviv. The
damage it sustained during the assault was then
estimated by a member "as equal in value to an
entire year of work." The heroism can never be
overrated. Shelled by tanks and artillery and
bombed from the air, valiant Hatzor stopped the

Egyptians in their tracks and held them until the new Israel army swept southwards in its drive towards Beersheba. The Second World War experience of the Americans, and that gained in the Hagana by the Sabras, stood Hatzor and the rest of Israel in good stead.

CHAPTER IX

Variation

Hatzor, third American kibbutz of Hashomer Hatzair, preceded the Habonim kibbutz, Gesher Haziv, by one year. Started in 1948, Gesher Haziv it will be recalled, is the kibbutz that made its fame nationally because of its revolt against patterns of family life and education held sacred by most of the kibbutz movement. If the moshav shitufi lies sociologically somewhere between kibbutz and moshav, then Gesher Haziv — with its system of **lina mishpachtit** — represents a type of halfway house between kibbutz and moshav shitufi. At the time of writing, Urim in the Negev and Kfar Hanassi in Upper Galilee are changing over to this system.

The term **lina mishpachtit,** which means literally family sleeping, describes the system reintroduced by Gesher Haziv in its early years whereby children sleep in family housing with their parents at night. Although it was not the first kibbutz to introduce this system, Gesher Haziv nevertheless sparked a fiery discussion throughout the kibbutz movement by insisting on its innovation. The first collective Degania Aleph and later Ein Harod among others, originally experimented with the system many years before, but Gesher Haziv, first among hundreds of collectives since to try it again, renewed the controversy.

Penina Grader, then co-ordinator of the children's houses at the American village, first explained in an article in Hamekasher* why Gesher Haziv embarked upon the experiment. 1) Overcrowding prevents the younger child from having a corner of his own in which to play, and the older from having a quiet corner to read. 2) Going to bed under cramped conditions is a strain for the child instead of a source of relaxation. 3) The short daily period, during which parents come together with their children, often results in the parents' attempting to compensate both themselves and their children for what the latter have missed during the remainder of the day. This produces exaggerations, tensions, and a general lack of satisfaction.

Lina mishpachtit would provide children with greater intimacy, security and privacy in the family home. In reply to the argument that its system would invade the privacy and equality of the mother, reimposing upon her those very household chores against which the kibbutz originally revolted, Gesher Haziv expressed the view that the emancipation of the woman members is

* Then organ of the World Habonim movement.

to be found in the fact that she works as an equal partner with her male comrade the entire day, and is consequently separated from her children, which means that separation at night is not an integral and essential part of the process.

Gesher Haziv's answer was valid enough in so far as it referred to equality, based upon full economic participation in the collective, but there remained the problem of equality of opportunity in taking part in social and cultural life in the evenings after work hours. Experience and experiment presented their own reply. A system of "baby-sitting" developed, as often practiced among young couples in town, with the advantage that one person, or the older children, could watch over the infants of several homes simultaneously. All thought the price was little to pay against the increase of happiness and serenity produced by the entire family being together in the evening.

There was, of course, another development in the entire kibbutz movement to which Gesher Haziv pointed as justification for its experiment. Family life in the collective, as the average age went up, had begun to supersede that of the **chevra,** the community. When a kibbutz group started its existence with very young people and few children, its community life in this halcyon period was certainly intensive. When one, two and more children came, however, and parental energy declined with work and age, the restful solace of the family room became more and more in-

viting than endless community meetings and cultural circles. **Lina mishpachtit,** claimed Gesher
Haziv, was in line with the fundamentals of its life.

The discussion concerning **lina mishpachtit**
continued at Gesher Haziv for a full year. Not
the least important factor was the additional
building budget required, particularly as the kibbutz was young and still beset with post-natal
economic problems. Moreover, the **garin** that established Gesher Haziv was somewhat older than the
average. The average **garin** in fact does not have
children when it establishes a new settlement.
From its first day Gesher Haziv had to concern
itself with twenty-five children and hence housing, teachers, and services for them. It was the
presence of these children, however, so early in
its collective life that led Gesher Haziv to an
early decision about its educational and family
system. The year-long discussion, during which
all building operations were held up, ended in an
overwhelmingly majority vote in favor of permanent family housing with children's rooms. The
decision to postpone building had been wise as
otherwise large sums of money would have been
needed to convert standard kibbutz housing into
suitable accommodation. In fact a number of settlements preparing to follow Gesher Haziv's lead
later admitted that this practical problem was one
of the important reasons they had not yet done
so.

In other ways, Gesher Haziv operates as other
kibbutz villages. Its children live in their own

community by day, eat and study together, the
kibbutz providing their clothing and all other services. Nevertheless, there are not a few members
of the kibbutz movement who are of the view
that this first and natural step towards a more
intimate and integrated family life may be
followed by others that will bring many kibbutzim to the moshav shitufi way of life. But most
say the kibbutz essentials are collective
ownership of the economy, the community labor
pool and the equal sharing of profits. Village differences, such as the family and not the community becoming the pivot of existence, are a matter
of socialist choice.

To Habonim in America, the group that founded Gesher Haziv represented a departure in another way. Hitherto, as noted earlier, that movement had sent individuals and small groups to
Palestine to join established settlements. This was
the first time that members of the movement had
decided to form a **garin** in America which, like
the **kibbutz aliya** of Hashomer Hatzair, would
follow through by establishing its own settlement
point. The Gesher Haziv group that formed such
a **garin** had met in conference for the first time
in New York during the Hanuka Festival of
1946. Although it did not then formulate precise
plans, a permanent framework was established.
An executive committee was elected to work out
plans for the **garin's** first forty members.

The first large group of Garin Aleph, as Habonim called its kibbutz nucleus, arrived for

training in April 1948 at Ramat Yochanan on the
very day that that settlement was attacked by
Arab military units, the vanguard of the large-
scale invasion that was to follow the forth-
coming proclamation of Israel as a State. In a
matter of months the American group had
reached 80 in number and after less than a year
of training at Ramat Yochanan it united with a
group of 40 Sabras from Kibbutz Beth Haarava
and settled its own land. The site was on the
coastal plain between the city of Haifa and the
Lebanese border. A description by one of the settlers reads:

> "Make no mistake, we're at Gesher Ha-
> ziv, a spot with a view that's worth millions
> — the Mediterranean on the west, the hills
> of Lebanon on the north, the hills of Gali-
> lee on the east, and the 'palisade' view of
> Haifa on the south. Our beach is about one
> mile in length and about one hundred yards
> wide, with natural lagoons ideally suited for
> wading for children. Our land is bounded on
> the north by a very large wadi (dry river
> bed) called Wadi Salik. We own, or rather
> lease from the J.N.F. 875 acres of land and
> have our own well which supplies us with
> approximately 50,000 gallons of water an
> hour."

The Sabra group with which the Americans had
united had evacuated a famous kibbutz that had
gained world-wide renown for its experiments in
land reclamation on the saline northern shore
of the Dead Sea. Their kibbutz was overrun by

the Arab Legion and its buildings were razed to
the ground. The conquerors uprooted its plants
and trees and returned utter desolation to the
place. When the war ended, its site remained in
Jordanian hands. Forty members of this Beth
Haarava group joined the Americans at Gesher
Haziv.

The land of the new West Galilee kibbutz was
wooded and on it were growing orange, fig, apri-
cot, olive and peach trees most of which had to be
uprooted because of their placement. These
had been left by their Arab owners who had fled
during the war. Years of work went into the
uprooting, bulldozing, and planting, stone-clearing
and gathering stumps, branches and roots. According to the Agricultural Department of the
Government this was the longest land-clearing
project carried out by any kibbutz. In fact, in
1959 for the first time could it be said that Gesher
Haziv was cultivating all of its arable land —
and settlement day was January 27, 1949.

By 1959 the kibbutz had 500 acres of its land
under irrigation, of which 100 consisted of orange
groves, 75 of banana plantations and the remainder
of crops like sugar beets, vegetables and pasture.
Field crops consisted of wheat, rye, sorghum and
hay. A successful experiment was conducted raising
peppers and cucumbers under plastic cover to induce early growth, making them marketable early
in the season. Industrial crops such as cotton and
peas for canning were planted. The poultry houses
were yielding 7,000 eggs per day.

By summer 1962 the economy of Gesher Haziv
was based mainly on its bananas (1000 tons per
year), oranges, cotton, potatoes and turkeys. The
turkey farm, one of the largest in the country and
next to that of Beth Herut in size, was hatching
and breeding for sale some 30,000 birds per year.
A plan was being considered to develop a sausage
industry and build a deep-freeze plant. Another
auxiliary industry was the Gesher Haziv Guest
House, a hotel which accommodates 90 people. Another project, evoking pride among members, was
the Regional High School located at Gesher
Haziv to which neighboring settlements such as
Hanita, Metzuba, Beth Haemek and Rosh-Hanikra
were sending their children. Gesher Haziv is today
the site of the Habonim Workshop, the year-long
study and work project of American Habonim in
Israel.

Many of the early members of the kibbutz knew
no Hebrew when they arrived in the country. The
transition from English was not easy and at first
general meetings were held in both languages. As
more and more Americans developed a working
knowledge of Hebrew, the meetings shifted to that
language, although for some time a "translation
table" had to be maintained. Today, although English is still heard in private conversation, and English periodicals and books are read by many, Hebrew is no longer a problem, and used at general
gatherings and everyone reads the Hebrew press.

One of the features of the settlement's cultural
life is its Little Theatre Group. Gesher Haziv

has also an excellent choir, square-dancing groups, a botany circle, and a myriad of Hebrew, English, literature and other classes and discussion circles.

One of the village's major preoccupations is with "Jewish tradition in cultural life". In part this reflects a more general problem in the country as a whole. For several years now services have been conducted on the High Holidays, at first because a number of parents lived in the settlement but more recently in response to the demand of members as well. Many of the children attend these services, a factor which may be the result of the village's family system.

Menucha Kraines, a member of Gesher Haziv, in 1959 summed up this development thus:

> "What will be the future development of this trend? It is impossible to predict at present. What is clear is that there is a strong desire in the kibbutz to find some form of Jewish expression. This desire, which exists in many places, is given special impetus in Gesher Haziv, where the population consists of a large number of Anglo-Saxons who came from communities where there are strong ties to Jewish traditions and customs, which have found expression not only in the Orthodox manner. In addition, there are many non-Americans who were educated as Orthodox Jews. Although they put aside Orthodox ritual, they want something to replace it. What that 'something' will be, perhaps the next ten years will tell."

CHAPTER X

Ein Dor

November 29, 1947 is a date in Jewish history which will retain its lustre forever. On that day over two-thirds of the representatives of the United Nations General Assembly voted in favor of a Jewish State. Jews in Palestine rejoiced, local Arabs received the news in anger and began a strike. In a matter of days war against Palestinian Jewry began with attacks on villages, lines of communication and strategic positions to forestall the establishment of Israel.

The British, charged to hand the country over peacefully, exhibited a partiality towards the Arabs that verged upon support. They left borders open to the penetration of invading military units from the surrounding Arab countries. They continued to supply weapons to these countries under previous agreements and pacts. They attempted to disarm and curtail the Hagana. Their naval blockade was maintained against Jews moving from displaced persons' camps to Palestine.

At the center of the clash between Palestine Jewry and the British was the struggle for im-

migration. In fact the very demand for Jewish
sovereignty was the outcome of British refusal
to permit the free entry of Jews to their National
Home. The frontline, as far as the Hagana was
concerned, was the Mediterranean where a constant stream of battered, leaky tramp ships and
other decrepit vessels sought to evade British de-
stroyers, cruisers, aircraft and radar posts and
bring their weary human cargoes of homeless
Jews to Palestine's shores.

Some of the immigrant vessels were caught
and their passengers herded into British intern-
ment camps on the island of Cyprus. Others successfully ran the blockade, landing at chosen
beaches. It was a vast and daring undertaking,
dubbed by the British "illegal immigration", or
in Hebrew by the Jews as **aliya beth.** It was
conducted by the sea arm of the Hagana's com-
mando force, the Palmach. The arm itself was
called Pal-Yam.

The British refusal to permit free entry of
Jews to Palestine also affected members of Western pioneer youth movements. Those who grew to
maturity during World War II and wished to em-
igrate or were now released from the armies of
the United Nations sought means of reaching
Palestine. A decision was taken that they should
join the stream of European "illegals" who were
boarding the blockade runners off the coasts of
southern France and Italy. As the human traffic
moving from Russia, Poland, other East European
countries and Germany as well reached a vast

scale, many Western pioneers volunteered their
services to the **aliya beth,** and for periods of six months and more worked in the em-
barkation camps and on the ships carrying the
immigrants.

As many of the vessels were purchased and
refitted in American shipyards, and had first to
be sailed across the Atlantic, members of the
pioneer movements who had had nautical training
during World War Two in the navy or merchant
marine volunteered as crews. Many of the sailors
of so famous a ship as "Exodus", for example,
were American **chalutzim.** A high percentage of
all "illegal" immigrants to Palestine during this
period were transported by ships manned by such
American crews. The vessels involved were Wedg-
wood, Hagana, Arlosoroff, Ben Hecht, Hatikva,
Theodor Herzl, Exodus 1945, Geula, Medinat
Hayehudim, Kibbutz Galuyot and Atzmaut. 40%
of the "illegals" of this period entered Israel on
ships manned by American crews.

After encounters with British naval vessels,
many of the blockade runners were interned in Cyprus with their refugee charges. Those
that got through turned their ships around and
made other runs. When duty was completed, the
demobilized sailors, engineers and other crewmen
ended up in Palestine, themselves "illegal" immigrants, as members of new groups preparing to
establish pioneer villages or of settlements already established. When full-scale Arab war was
launched after the establishment of Israel on

May 14, 1948, they continued the immigration
traffic and added to it the task of bringing in vital
supplies and ammunition and establishing a navy.
As their Israel war service, many of these veterans of the **aliya beth** struggle returned to
the sea until independence was secured.

The story of Western participation in **aliya
beth,** the naval war and Machal* has yet to be
told. The number that took part totalled hundreds,
their qualitative role was of inestimable value.
Few Palestinians had been afforded the opportunity during the World War of specialized naval
training. Moreover, in addition to the dangers
involved running the British naval blockade, the
Westerners had to evade the scrutiny and pros-
ecution of the authorities in England and America as well.

Among the Americans who sailed the ships
are members of Kfar Blum, Gesher Haziv, Maayan
Baruch, Ein Dor, Sasa and Beth Herut. Maayan Baruch, a kibbutz in Upper Galilee, near
Kfar Blum, was founded by South African and
Sabra pioneers in 1947 as a link in the chain of
frontier settlements that acted during the Arab-
Israel war as a shield for the whole Huleh Valley.
A small group of members of American Habonim
joined Maayan Baruch during this period, some
of whom were the sailors of the **aliya beth**
epic. There are six members of this American
group still in Maayan Baruch.

* Mitnadvei Chutz Laaretz (overseas volunteers).

The sailors and other members of the American village of Ein Dor began to arrive in the country at the end of 1946 and headed for Mishmar Haemek for their pre-settlement training. In the course of the following three years, some 75 additional members of the **kibbutz aliya** (Daled) to which they belonged assembled, and with their partners, were ready to establish Kibbutz Ein Dor, within sight of the famous mountain of Tabor. These American veterans of World War Two in fact established the first kibbutz that was to occupy its land during the actual fighting of Israel's War of Independence.

Their partners consisted of Sabras and German immigrant youth from the local Hashomer Hatzair whose group was called Kibbutz Aliya Vav. The immigrants, trained in the country as youngsters by Youth Aliya, had joined with the Sabras in 1940 and together had formed the **atzmaut** point near Hadera. At that time they numbered but 35 and hence, soon after, Vav began to look around for reinforcements. At Nachlat Yehuda, a small group of Hungarian members of their movement had established an **atzmaut** point of its own but it, too, realized its forces were insufficient to contemplate building a kibbutz. The Vav group moved to Nachlat Yehuda and it was during this stage that the Americans training at Mishmar Haemek made first contact with them.

The decision to establish a single kibbutz group out of this assortment of people from Germany, Hungary, Israel, the United States and Canada was no simple one for the Americans. Nor was it, of course, for their partners either. In negotiations for such unions, however important the ideological and political affinities of the prospective partners may be, these are not the decisive immediate considerations. These are factors taken for granted, otherwise such negotiations would never begin.

Among the immediate factors taken into account is the average age of the potentially united group as a whole as this may determine the choice of a settlement site. For example, a young kibbutz with a low average age, somewhere between 18 and 21, is likely to settle on a dangerous, exposed border region where conditions — both agricultural and defense — are at their toughest. In contrast, a group whose members are mostly 25 and upwards is likely to be offered a place to build its kibbutz where one or both of these conditions are easier. "Easier", in this sense, must be understood as a relative term meaning a little less tough, and should not be confused with settlement conditions outside the kibbutz sector. For all kibbutzim have a rough beginning.

Ein Dor began its life with 50 children. These were, of course, not all the offspring of the Americans. The age of the partners was also relatively high in pioneer terms. The Sabras and German youth were of the same "advanced" age as the Americans, since they had started life as a kibbutz nucleus as early as 1946. Hence when the

first group went to Ein Dor proper, the mothers and
children remained at Nachlat Yehuda until permanent accommodation could be erected. Naturally,
from the start, this imposed a heavy financial
burden on the new village. A large part of initial
budgets, covered by loans, had to be allocated
at the outset to housing, under decent conditions,
these first fifty children, and providing for them
adequate social and educational services. Apart
from budget it also involved substantial manpower.

The economy of the kibbutz had actually
started, in embryonic form, at Nachlat Yehuda.
A modern lime-burning kiln, the first furnace of
its kind in the country, had been set up there.
Three heavy trucks had been bought as the kibbutz shares in a local haulage cooperative. At
Beth Dagon land had been leased for truck farming. The remainder of the group's income at
that stage was derived from wage labor in nearby
groves and in building. These sources of income
were maintained whilst the vanguard sent to Ein
Dor began working on the permanent site, and
even when progress was made and all members
moved to Ein Dor, these activities, plus long-term,
low interest loans from the Jewish Agency
Settlement Department, the Workers' Bank (Bank
Hapoalim) of the Histadrut and other sources,
enabled the young settlement to begin its development work and provide its members with a
minimum standard of living until it had produce
to sell.

Low living standards at the beginning and settlement itself at a time of war were not the only problems that faced the American group. As had other from Western countries, its members suffered during the first five years from a basic cultural disadvantage. The Sabras used Hebrew as their mother tongue. The German and Hungarian members of the group had come to the country as youth and hence had grown up in its Hebrew culture. The Americans could not assume their due share of responsibility in the organization of Ein Dor's internal cultural life or in its outside contacts. Nor was it easy for them, during this period of physical hardship, to study a new language so entirely different from their own.

Joint creation, however, has powerful therapeutic value. It diminishes distance between people and creates a common legacy of tradition and experience. This is particularly apparent in the case of kibbutz communities, however heterogeneous, and Ein Dor was no exception. In the course of the process of joint evolution, the positive standards of both Americans and Sabras manifested themselves and these can be discerned in today's Kibbutz Ein Dor. As to its generation of youngsters now growing up in the village, it is almost impossible to detect in any of them the distinct "ethnic" characteristics of their parents. In some cases a superior knowledge of English in the classroom is the only clue.

As to Ein Dor itself, the village has an at-

tractive appearance. Entry through its main gate
soon brings the traveler face to face with the
green of extensive, lawns, the red splash of flowers, exotic sub-tropical trees and a large prefabricated dining hall, (supplied as standard
equipment to the young kibbutz of today by the
settlement authorities). A tall and impressive
watertower, with a symbolic candelabra on its
top, overlooks the village. From the lawn and
through the windows of the dining hall can be
seen the arched mound that is Mount Tabor,
shaded midway by a whisker of trees, and sur-
mounted by its Franciscan monastery which from
the distance seems to tilt to one side.

Near the dining hall is a unit almost standard today, the soda dispenser. Another pleasant
touch is the espresso-type bar housed in a tasteful
club-room where members relax and have coffee or
tea each free evening. Its colorful formica-topped
tables and stools are gay, as are the paintings
by kibbutz artists hung around the room, and
the entire atmosphere is warm and cordial. Periodicals, a radio, chess-sets and a phonograph add
their attractions to this recent kibbutz institution.

The village swimming pool was built not long
ago at a cost of I.L.60,000 from German restitution money paid to members of German origin
all of whom turned every mark into the community treasury. It is one of the loveliest pools in the
country, certainly of the kibbutz chain. Surrounded by green lawns, it is divided into sec-

tions for toddlers, children and adults and has
all the diving-boards, slides and other equipment
one expects to find in more luxurious surroundings.

Housing in Ein Dor, reflecting the various
stages of its groups' history, ranges from primitive huts to the latest "cottage" type family
unit, with two rooms on different levels. One
innovation, is the centrally-heated water fed to
every home. One of the village landmarks is a
real cottage, a house of three rooms situated in
a beautiful garden which was built after work
hours by one member who lugged its stones from
a deserted Arab village nearby. As insufficient
radios existed, Ein Dor fitted all its family units
with speakers and a choice of three programs daily
are available to listeners through this "piped"
source. The kibbutz has added a fourth program
in the form of its own "station" — Kol Ein Dor.*

The economy of the village is still exclusively
agricultural although members are at present
looking around for an auxiliary enterprise, "something for which market prospects are good and
which will employ hands off-season." Farm land
consists of 1,750 acres, 500 of them used as natural pasture, the remainder employed to grow
field crops, wheat, oats, sorghum, sugar beets and
cotton and such fruit as apples, peaches, apricots,
pears, grapes and citrus. The dairy has 120 milk-

---

* As we go to press, we learn that Ein Dor is
now supplying its members with radios.

ers, with a high average yield of 6,300 litres annually per cow. Poultry for meat and eggs numbers 13,000 birds. There are 600 head of sheep.
Besides its haulage trucks, the kibbutz does contract work with a shoveldozer and bulldozer. It
has also mechanized carpentry and machine shops.
Annual turnover by 1962 had reached $433,333
whilst village investments by that date were valued at over a million.

The main farm problem of Ein Dor, from its
very beginning until the present day, has been
water. Three drillings have so far been made
but all have yielded nothing but highly saline
water. The Mekorot Company pumps some saline
water and a limited quantity of sweet from the
Kfar Baruch reservoir but this must somehow be
increased. The second headache facing the community is manpower shortage, resulting from the
fact that half of its adults work in the village
services.

Total population in 1962 numbered 550 of
whom 205 were actual members, 220 were children, the remainder consisting of training groups
and parents of members. The village has built a
high school for its own children and for the 20
trainees of Aliyat Hanoar receiving their mixture
of academic and vocational education there. These
youngsters are from Poland and Rumania and,
with the kibbutz offspring, the school population
is 120 students.

Of the original group of 75 Americans, 50
remain as village veterans. One of them summed

up surviving American characteristics of Ein Dor
as: "Baseball, an easy-going manner, straight-
forwardness, less tension about politics, a highly
conscious egalitarianism." Life, all agree, is busy.
There is a choir of 50 people, a dramatic group
that keeps putting on plays of all national origins
and the home-made radio program. One of the
members, Moshe Siklai, a plumber by day, is a
highly valued sculptor. And, of course, there are
the study groups and lectures, mostly through
the winter.

CHAPTER XI

Sasa and Barkai

Fifth in the chain of American kibbutz villages established by Hashomer Hatzair is Sasa. It was set amid high mountain peaks and deep valleys, about five miles from the Meron crossroads on the way from Tarshicha to Safed. Exposed in the winter months to cold, rain and at times snow, villages in this beautiful area enjoy a pleasant and temperate summer. The enchanting Galilean scenery, crowned by the mountaintop town of Safed within easy reach, has made Sasa a point of pilgrimage for thousands of American and local tourists since its foundation in 1949.

Not far from Sasa is the large Arab village of Gush Halav, near the site of Gisshala, famous since Roman times when one of its inhabitants, John, together with Simon Bar Giora, led the Zealot revolt in 66 C.E.* In short, the entire environment of Kibbutz Sasa is a maze of historical and archeological sites, an area of mysticism and

* The revolt became a bloody war and it ended with the destruction of the Temple in 70 C. E.

religious pilgrimage and, because of magnificent
mountain scenery, a mecca for artists. Perhaps
out of respect for or awe of this unusual heri-
tage, the initiators of Sasa decided to build
their village out of hewn stone so that it would
blend with the landscape and not stand out like
a sore thumb as do many with their white
plastered walls, red roofs, concrete and glass.

The choice of the site certainly could not
have been dictated by agricultural considerations,
for Sasa has a notorious and dire shortage of
cultivable land. On the hillside much of the area
is rock-strewn and thinly covered with earth.
The valley nearby is good for deciduous fruit
orchards but limited in area. The planners who
decided where Sasa would settle were obviously
influenced by strategic considerations for the
ridge of mountains overlooking the village and
extending across this northern extremity of Israel from west to east separates the country
from Lebanon. Sasa in fact is one of a protective
chain established to block invasion and dis-
courage infiltration.

The mountainous terrain upon which the village was established has determined the shape
of Sasa's difficult economy. Its valley land has
apples, plums, peaches, pears and vines whilst
in recent years, soil reclaimed from the marshes
of the Huleh Valley below has been given to the
kibbutz to grow its fodder crops. To supplement
its fruit growing and other branches, carp-
breeding ponds have also been developed in the

valley. The fodder crops are for Sasa's beef herd
of 200 head of cattle and its 45 milkers. The village also has large poultry houses which appear
to jut out of the hillside from the road below and
it owns a share in the local bus cooperative.

Sasa's population in 1962, some 13 years after
its birth, is still limited in number. It includes
100 members and some 55 children. The remainder, consisting of training groups, Aliyat Hanoar
(Youth Aliya) and members' parents, bring the
number of total inhabitants to over 300. The
reason they are not more, and village members do
not try to hide this, is that they have had a
constant turnover. When the village began, its
founders consisted of 90 Americans whose ambi-
tion had been originally to establish a village
solely of people from the United States. This, it
will be recalled, had been the earlier dream of
the founders of Ein Hashofet. Today, only 30
Americans (including three Canadians) remain.
Other kibbutz members, 65 in number, are the
members of three different Sabra groups that
joined the Americans in 1953, 1957 and in 1962.

Some of the Americans at Sasa were not only
veterans of World War II, they had also participated in aliya beth, the movement of Jewish
refugees across Europe to Palestine in defiance
of the British. Here were forged some of the
ties that led them to Sasa.

Most of the Americans who "passed through"
the village returned to the United States. Most
of them left Sasa between the years 1949 and

1953, the most difficult ones not only for the kibbutz but for Israel as a whole. During that period the country suffered from its greatest shortages, particularly of food supplies. Even potatoes and other vegetables were rationed at the worst period. The shortage was of course the result of Israel's absorption, during the first five years of its independence, of over 700,000 immigrants. Production of food and other items, now more than adequate in most cases, lagged behind population increase.

This situation, in the towns in particular, must have deterred not a few Americans from attempting to settle elsewhere in the country when they left their kibbutz. Nor did employment opportunities exist then as they do today.

One of the reasons for this unfortunate experience of Sasa may be the unilaterally American nature of its original group. Integration into the new Hebrew culture of the country is certainly not promoted by living in an American island in Israel. And such integration is absolutely essential, as by itself, the task of building a village — in the case of Sasa a most demanding task — is not enough to lead people to strike root.

The change in Sasa's fortunes may be marked from the absorption of the first Sabra complement or reinforcement **(hashlama)** group. There could have been no better incentive to its American members to study Hebrew and draw closer to the rest of Israel. Moreover, as in the case of

Ein Dor, the interaction of cultures, although not without tensions, may bring out the best in the partners. This is particularly true against a background of joint endeavor and creativity.

Departures of members from a pioneer group are depressing. They also have an opposite effect. Those that remain seem to draw together more closely in greater determination. The same may be said of the Sabra groups who joined the settlement. The community of 100 members of today are the solid and "battle-scarred" veterans who are most unlikely to seek any other form of life. How much the kibbutz will grow in the future is to no small extent dependent upon its economic possibilities.

As to its present situation, one of Sasa's members commented recently: "Almost all key positions in the economy are occupied by Americans. The secretary of Sasa is from the United States, the leader of the fruit orchard branch is also an American. This is due to the greater experience gained over a longer period by the Americans. They are also older than the Sabras of the settlement. Today, more Hebrew is used than English, a development helped greatly by the Sabras. Our library is now half Hebrew, half English, also a marked change..."

Americans in Sasa also play a leading role in the cultural life of the village. This is not surprising as "almost all of them had a university background, whilst most of the Sabras stopped their studies on completion of high school". A

problem in Sasa, exclusively American, is that
of visits home to parents. The Sabras, of course,
are never far from home. The kibbutz has made
possible at least one visit back to the United
States for each of its American members, no mean
feat and a considerable budgetary strain. It is a
problem that faces all pioneer villages with members from Western countries.

* * *

As the Americans of Sasa started their village
in 1949 amid the hills of Upper Galilee, the first
members of the next **kibbutz aliya** (Vav) of
Hashomer Hatzair in the United States reached
Israel. The new arrivals, eight in number, proceeded for training to the kibbutz Kfar Masaryk,
located in the Zevulun Valley. During the year
the small group made contact with another nucleus, training at Ein Hamifratz, the kibbutz next
door. This nucleus consisted of twelve South African members of the movement who had few
prospects of reinforcement. Hence, at Ein Hamifratz, the South Africans decided to join the American **kibbutz aliya** which, all told, **numbered 150** members. By the time the Americans left Kfar Masaryk they numbered 30 and,
together with a second nucleus of their **kibbutz
aliya** (training at Kibbutz Mesilot) and the
South Africans, they had ready for settlement in
1950 a total of 60 people. One year later, a third
nucleus of Kibbutz Aliya Vav, consisting of
40 members, arrived to join them.

By 1950, the decision had been made to unite

the American **kibbutz aliya** with a group of
Rumanian and Hungarian pioneers of Hashomer
Hatzair. This European group had come into being
when its members were interned together in a
camp on Cyprus by the British who had inter-
cepted their respective **aliya beth** ships. After
their release, the members of this united group
called Bnei Avoda spent a year training in
veteran settlements and in 1949 they were given
land on which to build a kibbutz in Wadi
Ara. As a group of 100 people they were considered sufficient in number to begin establishing
a new settlement point.

Not all of the Bnei Avoda group had been
members of the youth movement Hashomer Hatzair in Europe. Some, without such a background, had joined the kibbutz nucleus when in
Cyprus. Nor were all of the first settlers at Barkai in 1949 Rumanians or Hungarians. During
the training period a small group of Polish pioneers, also not large enough to settle on their
own, joined Bnei Avoda. Hence, when the
union with the Americans and South Africans was
made, this mixture of Rumanians, Hungarians
and Poles had already the first year on their
settlement site behind them. By 1950, therefore,
Kibbutz Barkai had a population of 160 and the
prospects of further reinforcement by approximately 100 Americans yet to come.

Barkai's settlement site, off the main Wadi
Ara road, was once the feudal estate of Abdul
Hadi, whose sons today figure prominently in

the Jordanian Government. The Abdul Hadi residence, a tall, flat-roofed house of stone built
in Turkish times, still towers as a landmark over
the kibbutz. From it, to the west, can be seen
Gan Hashomron and the mountains of Gilboa, and
to the east the Jordan border. The house is today
being converted into a museum by Barkai as the
kibbutz has already unearthed many valuable ar-
chaelogical relics of the chalcolithic, Hyksos and
Israelite periods.

These finds are constantly being dug up.
Each time the village adds to its housing area
burial caves and catacombs are discovered and,
once again, the Department of Antiquities is called in to study the site. The finds, according to
law, belong to the Department, but its representatives have been tactful and understanding enough
to agree that the kibbutz should retain a part of
them for exhibition in its own museum. Some of
the village members are keen students of ar-
chaelogy and handle the finds   professionally,
hence mutual confidence exists. Among the dis-
coveries so far have been an assortment of jars,
pots and other vessels, lamps, weapons and coins.
Much more is expected as the kibbutz proceeds
with its program of modern construction.

From the tower of the Hadi house the rich
valley land of the kibbutz reaches out below
towards the modern highway, built upon the
same route that once linked Egypt and Babylon.
In fact Barkai itself sits on a rise which was
undoubtedly a caravan station and burial place

of successive civilizations reaching far back into antiquity. A natural stream flows by, providing water the entire year round. A tel near Barkai is thought to contain the remains of the Biblical town of Arabot, one of twelve administrative centers in the days of King Solomon. Archaeological exploration has not yet begun at this site. As in the days of antiquity, modern Barkai is a strategic point dominating the Afula-Hadera-Jerusalem highway which, in the period of the British Mandate, passed through Arab Tulkarm.

The land holdings of Barkai total 3,000 acres, of which 2,000 are good bottom soil. The rest is spread over rocky hills. All of the good land is now under irrigation and fruit, cotton and vegetables flourish on it. In 1962, for example, fruit plantations included 50 acres of bananas, 55 acres of citrus, 38 acres of avocados, 12.5 acres each of apples and grapes. Over 100 acres of cotton had been planted and, near it, were 50 acres of corn. Besides potatoes (20 acres) and other vegetables, the farm economy also included 800 head of sheep, 80 milch cows, 30 calves and poultry for breeding purposes, meat and eggs. Further income was being derived from kibbutz shares in the Gal Am sugar refinery and from a local transport cooperative.

In its first five years of life as a community, Barkai sustained heavy losses in membership. Many of the Rumanians and Hungarians, as already mentioned, had not had movement background or training before they joined the kibbutz

in Cyprus. Under the pressures of early pioneer
and collective life this weakness was soon exposed. For example, from the earliest days, sharp
discussions developed between them and the Americans over such basic kibbutz issues as collective
ownership of essential property and work discipline. The Americans, dedicated as they were to
kibbutz principles, were rightly adamant about
such fundamentals. Within a short time, it was
noted, the Rumanian members were, without
exception, concentrated in all the non-agricultural
branches of work in the village, whilst the Americans virtually took over the farm economy.

During this difficult period, the kibbutz lost 34
people in its first year of settlement life. By
1955, of the 60 Rumanians and Hungarians of
the original Bnei Avoda group, only 30 were
left. By 1960, there were only 20. Of the 40
members of the Polish group that had united
earlier with Bnei Avoda, 9 remained at Barkai by that date. The American group had also
its losses. Of its entire kibbutz aliya of 150
people, approximately two-thirds left the group.
Hence, in 1962, Barkai's population consisted of
140 members, including 53 Americans, 120 children and 7 parents. By that date the oldest children were 14 and were attending the district high
school at Ein Shemer.

Half of the Americans who left Barkai remained in Israel. Those who gave up during the
shortages and rationing of Israel's tsena period
(1950-1953), in most cases soon returned to the

United States. The half who settled down in
Israel's towns did so from 1955 onwards. Those
that stayed in the kibbutz not only assumed a
leading role in its economic life but also soon
assumed a prominent position in its cultural and
intellectual leadership as well. This, in retrospect,
was an inevitable development as none of the
European members had had the opportunity to
attend university while, of the Americans, all had
finished high school, most had attended college.

Necessity being the mother of invention, the
Americans had to work hard at their Hebrew
from the earliest days of Barkai. Assumption of
responsibility, as well as the need to have a common language among all elements, required this.
Moreover, when children began to talk, the kibbutz took a decision that parents should speak
to them only in Hebrew. A further incentive was
provided when an immigrant **ulpan** was started
by the settlement authorities at the village. This
type of intensive, concentrated six-month Hebrew
course for newcomers has taught the language
efficiently to hundreds of thousands of people
throughout the country. The course at Barkai has
facilities at each session for 35. Another incentive
developed when the settlement agreed to take a
group of 21 teen-agers of Youth Aliya for school-
ing and vocational training.

An innovation at Barkai, incidentally, which
in part answers the objections of the members of
Gesher Haziv about children sleeping separately
from parents is the telephone system it has devel-

They started arriving in Israel in the year 1950 as graduates of a small pioneer group in the United States called Plugat Aliya. It had come into being when senior members of Junior Hadassah, Massada and Young Judea decided to form jointly in Israel a kibbutz that represented their particular political point of view. All three organizations were affiliates of the General Zionist grouping in the United States and Israel which is a democratic, conservative wing of World Zionism. However, it is dedicated in principle to the concept of cooperation between labor and capital in the upbuilding of the National Home and hence sees nothing irreconcilable in its belief that it should establish its own kibbutz chain there.

The ideology of the kibbutz sector of the General Zionists is broad and "all-embracing". As a result, the cohesion that emerges from strong mutual and clear-cut socialist convictions was lacking among the Americans of Plugat Aliya, even though all were resolved to establish a united kibbutz. The first trainees of the training farm at Wappinger Falls, near Poughkeepsie, went to Kibbutz Ginnegar for pre-settlement experience. By the time 40 of them had gathered there it was decided that a union should be made with an Israel group — part Sabra, part Europeans trained in the country — of the local movement Maccabi Hatzair. The union, when land was made available for settlement, hence numbered 80 people. The Americans, most of them 25, were a few years older than their partners.

The Israel partner at the time of the union had been living in a moshava (rural settlement) as an **atzmaut** group since 1948. When the Arabs invaded the country a number had been called up into the new Israel Army. Some were killed in the fighting, and at Hasolelim today there is a memorial by the noted sculptor Yehuda Shemi of Kibbutz Kabri, dedicated to the fallen. A number of the Americans also fought in the War of Independence in the army and air force.

The first group to occupy the settlement site at Zippori (Sephoris) was stirred by its great natural beauty. It was summer of 1949, the days were moderately hot, the evenings cool. Members were also thrilled by the historic associations of their area. Here had been the meeting place of the Sanhedrin under Yehuda Hanassi after the Second Temple had fallen. At nearby Beth Netufa had been the fortress of Yodefet where Flavius Josephus had surrendered to the Romans. Zippori itself had been a large town and capital city of Herod Antipas' Ethnarchy in the first century. The settlers found on their land the ruins of ancient winepresses and, where Zippori stood, a number of graves.

Besides acquiring such scenic beauty and the echoes of history, the new settlers secured many much more practical advantages. The soil was rich and fertile, there was abundant water on the site. Nearby were fruit orchards that had been abandoned by the Arabs of Zafouriya, a town two miles away. As for trees, Hasolelim was

probably the first modern Hebrew village to inherit groves of sturdy oaks on its site, instead of
the hard, expensive task of afforesting the hillsides. Prospects were therefore good, but the beginning of Hasolelim was fraught with unusual
difficulties.

This period, according to Ben Nachum, "consisted of the days of **tsena** and during them the
group members, after four strenuous hours of
work each morning, ate half a hard-boiled egg
for their lunch." The low standard of
food, housing and everything else hit the
Americans hardest. The drop in their living standards was sudden and severe. "This affected the Americans more than anything else.
They knew there was always the road back to
the United States. Between 1949 and 1952 more
than half of them left the kibbutz and returned
to America. The Sabras also lost people. They,
too, had a haven of refuge in the cities with
their families. The Europeans of the Israeli group,
however, stuck it out as they had no place to
which to retreat."

Near the medical dispensary of Hasolelim
stand two huge eucalyptus trees, planted by the
Ben Nachums ten years ago. Members of the village have often suggested cutting them down as
they are in the area of new construction. The
Ben Nachums have steadfastly defended these
trees until now, perhaps because they symbolize
so profoundly their own roots in the village, sturdy and remarkable against a background of a

once strong group of Americans who numbered
one hundred.

* * *

Another sad story, from the viewpoint of
American settlement in Israel is that of Kibbutz
Yiftach. Once known as "the student kibbutz",
because members of the Inter-Collegiate Zionist
Federation of America (IZFA) joined with Sabras
to establish it on the Lebanese frontier, the village was torn by a sharp political division and
most of the American pioneers in it left. IZFA,
and its **chalutz** wing Haoleh, like the small
pioneer group Plugat Aliya lasted but a few
years. Neither had continuity, hence their first
pioneer groups to settle in kibbutzim in Israel
petered out without hope of reinforcement.

During its short life, IZFA, or rather Haoleh,
contributed to the consolidation of the then new
settlement of Yiftach. The frontier village of Yiftach came into being as a result of the merger of
two Israel partners, one including graduates
of the Mikve Israel Agricultural School for
boys and the Ayanot Training Farm for girls,
the other consisting of members of the Haifa
branches of the Hanoar Haoved youth organization of the Histadrut. While both Israel partners were receiving pre-settlement training at the
end of 1947, the fighting between Arabs and Jews
began that led to the outbreak of the Israel War of
Independence. The groups joined the Palmach,
striking force of the Hagana, and fought in the
Jezreel Valley, Western Galilee and Safed.

During the Galilee campaign the two groups made contact with each other as they were both in the same brigade, commanded by Yigal Alon. As the war continued, the brigade moved to the Negev for the campaign against the Egyptian army and after the liberation of the southern area they were transferred to Blaydah, not far from the Yiftach settlement site. There, on the Lebanese border, they fought their last engagement and then decided to establish their kibbutz. By 1950, a skeletal economy had been established.

In May 1951, the first members of IZFA arrived as a reinforcement group (hashlama) at Yiftach. They had completed their pre-settlement training at Kibbutz Beth Hashita and during that year had decided to maintain their "non-political" character as a group. This meant they intended to avoid affiliation with any of the three main parties of Israel's labor movement — Mapai, Mapam and Achdut Haavoda. The two last mentioned were at that time "united" as Mapam, although soon after they parted company. When a split occurred between the Mapai and Achdut Haavoda adherents within the Kibbutz Hameuchad, it was reflected in each individual kibbutz, and in Yiftach, had disastrous results for the American group, whose intentions had been to keep apart from political division. As the vanguard of a small and undefined movement, the Americans felt responsibility towards Haoleh for maintaining such political neutrality, regardless of how its individual members may have voted.

The net result was that most of the IZFA group, which originally had numbered 40, left the settlement for the towns or other places. A few remained in the original Yiftach, a few went with the remainder to Kibbutz Gadot. IZFA has since been superseded by the American Student Zionists Organization (S.Z.O.)

* * *

A third American pioneer nucleus, which had a short life, was the small group in the United States that called itself Hashavim. It was formed by members of the Labor Zionist Organization of America who after World War Two felt themselves too old and mature to be members of any of the existing pioneer youth movements in the United States. A few branches were established in New York and other cities and a first settlement group left for Israel at the beginning of 1951. It gathered at Kibbutz Kfar Giladi in Upper Galilee, until it numbered 30 people.

Already, in the parent kibbutz, it became clear that the Hashavim group had not the internal strength to become either a kibbutz nucleus in its own right or even maintain its unity and join a settled village as a reinforcement group. Some of its members objected to the full collectivism of the kibbutz pattern. They tended to favor the moshav shitufi. Others were undecided as to whether they should become a unit in a settled kibbutz and even those members who believed the Hashavim group should do this disagreed

as to which kibbutz or movement they should
go to.

Inevitably, the Hashavim nucleus at Kfar Giladi broke up. Some of its members joined Kibbutz
Gesher Haziv, some joined the moshav shitufi
Kfar Daniel, others Moshav Habonim. A few families joined Kfar Giladi itself. For several years
afterwards Hashavim sent small **aliya** groups to
Israel.

CHAPTER XIII

Kissufim – Negev Village

Although armistice agreements had been signed between Israel and the Arab States in 1949,
real peace was far from concluded. To the Arabs,
the agreements were but a pause before the
resumption of further hostilities. Not that the Arabs
were anxious to try a full test of strength again,
so soon after their painful and humiliating defeat.
Instead, they embarked upon limited warfare, such
as border raiding, infiltration, economic and political boycott and sea blockade. One of their
primary concerns was to prevent Israel from push-
ing ahead with its plans to settle and develop its
empty southern region, the Negev.

The armistice agreement signed with Egypt
(on the island of Rhodes) had left that country in
possession of the Gaza Strip, a long and narrow
finger of territory stretching northwards from
the old border between Sinai and Palestine along
the Mediterranean shore in the direction of Tel
Aviv. From this sliver of land raiding and occasional mortar and artillery bombardments were
undertaken, to deter Jewish settlers from establish-

ing new villages in the western Negev area. Israel in response decided to set up a protective
chain of settlements along its side of the Gaza
Strip border behind which development of agriculture and industry could proceed in relative
safety.

The type of village most suited to this role
of an agricultural and defensive outpost was,
naturally, the kibbutz. The thirty youngsters who
pitched their tents amid the desolate wasteland
in this area on March 1, 1951 were ideally suited to the role. All of them ex-servicemen of the
Arab-Israel war, later trained and toughened as
farmers in a veteran pioneer village, they now
assumed the task of settling on land less than
a mile from the Gaza Strip border. Between them
and the crisscrosses, trenches, bunkers and pill-
boxes of the Egyptian soldiers, were a few
haphazard markers bearing the reminder in Hebrew: "Here, Israel Ends".

The group, which began the kibbutz called
Kissufim, remained on this site awaiting reinforcement until April 1952, a period of thirteen
long months. It had little water and began dry
farming, planting 1,000 acres of dusty loess soil
(a mixture of clay and sand) with wheat and
barley, reminiscent of the patriarch Isaac who
did precisely this on the same Beersheba Plain.
The little water available was used sparingly
for household purposes and for a 10-acre plot of
vegetables. A dairy branch was started and
poultry acquired during the first settlement year.

The group was especially proud of its four tractors, two "cats" — the others wheel-type — and
housed them and other equipment in a primitive
shed, knocked together with wood and corrugated
sheeting. Next to it stood a lean-to garage for
servicing and repairs.

Accommodation then for Kissufim's founders
consisted of seven canvas tents. The sole solid
building was the concrete cube in which were
housed the generator and diesel motor, providing
electricity for light and power. Not far from the
tents stood the prefabricated dining shack, to one
end of which had been added a small hut-like extension that served as its kitchen. Not long before
their new members arrived, the first group at
Kissufim erected eight wooden prefabricated bungalows for themselves and their reinforcements.
Scattered here and there, at strategic spots, stood
small tin huts to serve as toilets and showers and
from them and the kitchen a network of thin
pipes passed over the surface of the dusty ground.
Such was Kissufim's encampment in the spring
of 1952. So poor was the kibbutz in those days,
that it was humorously given the sobriquet "Ein
Kessef" (without money), a nickname which has
been vanishing with the growing prosperity of
recent years.

Water was then scarce and precious in the
northern Negev. The sole supply, shared by the
first villages of the area, was drawn from the
Nir Am wells and was doled out with such a sparing
hand, that it entirely failed to meet requirements

other than the barest minimum needed for maintaining household and vegetable patch. Kissufim, for example, obtained through the 6-inch pipeline from Nir Am a total of 500 cubic meters daily. This pipeline, by the way, was the objective of the fiercest battles during the Egyptian invasion of 1948 for upon it depended existence itself for the first Negev villages. Nor was much relief provided by rainfall. The average, for this part of the country, in the best year, is twelve inches. There are not a few years when the total is much less.

Water shortage in 1952 was not Kissufim's only preoccupation. Despite the perimeter fence, made of miles of coiled barbed wire, equipped at regular intervals with arc lamps beamed outward, marauders from across the border struck for the first time. At night, taking cover in the ubiquitous wadis (watercourses, generally dry, but subject to winter flash floods), they stole not less than 60% of Kissufim's hard-earned harvest. "In those days," say the villagers, "we used too few people to guard our fields." At the end of 1952 infiltrators struck again — this time lifting 100 yards of 6-inch piping. From that night on, Kissufim increased its guards, mounted some on horseback for day patrol, and when darkness fell deployed them to cover its land as well as its encampment. A thirty-foot watchtower was erected, a red-roofed platform mounted on stilt legs from which the countryside could be kept under surveillance for miles around.

By the summer of 1953 the kibbutz started

putting up permanent buildings containing four rooms, each designed for a couple. Reinforcements from the United States, Canada, and a good number of the Latin American republics began to arrive. Among the newcomers was an engineer who had specialized in producing auto connecting rods and bearings. Starting with a small experimental workshop employing at most six people, this industry soon became an important income-earning adjunct to Kissufim's essentially agricultural economy. After machinery was acquired through the German Reparations Agreement with Israel, the workshop became a factory 400 square yards in floor area and was soon turning out spares for Willys Jeeps, Ford cars and trucks, and employing twenty workers permanently, even during the busy summer season.

The year 1955 was a very important one for Kissufim and the other villages of the area as during it the Yarkon-Negev water pipeline was completed. From a distance of 90 miles, a total of 90 million cubic metres of water per year began to be pumped through it. Kissufim benefited in that it could increase its irrigated area from 10 to 400 acres and was able to extend its agricultural horizon. Receiving 3,000 cubic meters of water daily, it was able to develop its fruit orchards which by 1956 included 12 acres of vine, 5 acres of plum trees. This beginning of fruit cultivation was initiated despite the pessimistic warnings of the "experts" who claimed that the soil and climate were unsuitable. Success in the

first year resulted in Kissufim expanding the area
allocated to fruit growing to 25 acres of grapes,
apricots, apples and plums.

Also in 1956 experiments were conducted with
other crops. The area, it should be emphasized,
had been wasteland for many centuries and its
new settlers had little prior experience or knowledge to guide them in their choice of crops.
They found that the linseed oil plant flourished
and sowed 200 acres with its seed. Five hundred
acres of mill corn were grown, 15 acres were planted with potatoes, 12 with peanuts, 1 with bananas
and 100 with canteloupe and water melons. The
dairy was also expanded from its original three
cows to 60 head, all of them a cross between
Dutch and American strains and housed in a
large, concrete building. The poultry section,
started with a few hundred birds, contained by
1956 over 3,500 white Leghorns, layers and broilers. The area and encampment of the village began to change in color from dun to green.

A comparison of the economic condition of
Kissufim in 1956 and 1962 reveals the remarkable
progress its settlers have made. Of its total land-
holding of 4,250 acres, 3,500 are now being used
to grow its grass and fodder crops. Under irrigation are 300 acres of cotton, sugar beet and potatoes. Its fruit orchards cover 57.5 acres of
land and include apples, peaches, plums, apricots
and grapes. The peach yield in 1962 was a national record, an extraordinary 18 tons per acre.
Kissufim had also in that year the highest cotton

yield in the area, a total of 1,920 kilograms per acre. The cotton department was then managed by a Brooklyn boy. In addition there were 70 acres of orange, grapefruit and lemon trees, due to bear their first fruit in 1963.

In the same six years, the increase in the village livestock was also impressive. Kissufim's poultry branch, for example, consisted of 50,000 birds by 1962, and produced 600,000 eggs per year and 90 tons of meat. The dairy had grown to 85 milkers and a total of 220 head of cattle. Milk production had reached 480,000 litres annually and an average of 6,300 litres per milker, about twelfth highest in the country. The annual turnover of the the entire economy was valued in 1962 at $416,666. Kissufim had 583 acres under cultivation, and was using 1,100,000 cubic meters of water per year, which was the maximum it was allowed by the regional water authorities. During drought years, however, the supply is far less and in fact Kissufim was hard hit between 1958 and 1962.

The encampment of Kissufim has meanwhile changed no less than its economy. By 1962 the number of permanent housing units constructed, of one and one-and-a-half rooms, had reached 70 and the following year a further 20 of two rooms each were to be added. In place of the small shack, a much larger prefabricated dining hall stood in the village center and to it a permanent kitchen was added in 1963 Soon, the dining hall itself will be replaced by a permanent structure. The year 1962 was one of intensive building. During it, the medical clinic was completed, as were the Culture House, the clothing store, steam laundry and three additional classrooms. Just the year before, the village celebrated the completion of its swimming pool, a vital necessity in the hot Negev climate, and a large 450-ton grain silo was also built.

As a community, Kibbutz Kissufim has since inception been a veritable "ingathering of the exiles". The group of thirty youngsters who first occupied the site included people from North and South America. They had in common sympathy with or membership in one of the pioneer youth movements named Dror-Hechalutz Hatzair. Once among the powerful pioneer movements of Eastern Europe, their precarious foothold in the Western hemisphere had been gained by émigré youth who had escaped the holocaust. Among the South American Jewish communities which have preserved their European and Yiddish culture in the midst of a well entrenched rather inhospitable Catholic environment, Dror-Hechalutz Hatzair has been able to develop a sizable movement. In the United States however where Jewry is much further removed from its East European origins, the movement started in 1946 and only after some abortive attempts to establish itself, gained a foothold.

The Americans and Canadians among the thirty founders of Kissufim included the earliest members of American Dror-Hechalutz Hatzair. A group

of 45 of them had volunteered to fight in Israel
when the Arabs invaded that country in 1948.
When the war ended they were demobilized from
Machal, as the overseas volunteers were called,
and decided to stay in the country, obtaining
pioneer training in a kibbutz in western Galilee
called Kabri. Of these 45 American servicemen,
27 are still in the kibbutz. While the Americans
and Canadians were training at Kabri, members
of the South American movement established a
kibbutz nucleus at Naan for pre-settlement training and during that year the two groups decided
to unite. The Americans thus transferred to Naan
from Kabri and from the union was chosen the
mixed group that occupied the site of Kissufim.

From this original thirty, the kibbutz population had grown by 1962 to 140 members, 120 children, 19 parents and 25 candidates. The last
mentioned usually live and work in a kibbutz for
a year after which they decide whether to join
the group permanently, and the kibbutz decides
whether they are suitable for membership. Including the Aliyat Hanoar training group num-
bering 38 youngsters, the population of Kissufim
today has been drawn from not less than 24
different countries. Of the members only 39 are
from the United States and Canada, 30 from South
America (Argentina, Chile, Brazil, and Uru-
guay), 30 from the Middle East (Iraq, Syria,
Lebanon, Egypt, Iran and Yemen). The rest come
from: Morocco, Tunisia, Poland, Russia, Rumania, Germany, Hungary, Austria, France and Ita-

ly. In addition, there are 28 Sabras. The average
age of the Americans is 29, and all but five of
them were born in the U.S.

One-sixth of the American members of Kissufim are teachers today (3 women and 2 men),
and one of these has been chosen to be principal of the high school opened in 1963. Its
student body consists of 20 children who have
grown up in Kissufim, plus a group of Youth
Aliya trainees. The irrigation expert of the settlement is one of its Canadian members, three
of the Americans work in the fruit orchards, the
village electrician and carpenter are Canadians.
The treasurer of the village in 1962 was from
the United States, as was its bookkeeper. The
village Secretariat at that date consisted of: 3
Americans, 2 Brazilians, 1 Sabra, 1 Pole, 1 Syrian (the Secretary).

As its variegated "ethnic" mixture suggests,
life in Kissufim shows the effect of different
influences. Diet is an excellent example. Meals
in the dining hall blend occidental and oriental
tastes. Kissufim, for instance, boasts that it is
the only kibbutz in the country that produces its
own home-made pizza and hummus*. When the
South Americans cook, their specialty is mutton
prepared Gaucho style, that is, over a fire made
in a pit, the sheep being roasted whole on the
hot coals. Besides their pizza, the Americans
have introduced apple pie. Everyone seems to

* Popular Near Eastern dish made of ground chick-
peas.

drink fabulous amounts of coffee. Shashlik has been made popular by Middle Easterners.

Hard as they work by day in the fields, members of the kibbutz seem to have a lot of energy to spare for evening cultural activities. The "spectator" brand consists of about 7 plays per year, performed by companies who come from Tel Aviv, 2 or 3 concerts and a monthly event such as a dance group or lecturer. Every year each member is entitled to a month of study — **yerach limud** — during which he works on the farm only half the day and studies during the second half and in the evening. The main topic chosen for the study month of 1962 was education. Two-thirds of the course consisted of lectures. Study groups active throughout the year chose such subjects as mathematics, Bible, agriculture and economics.

Apart from this formidable list, Kissufim has a dramatic group that last performed "The Doctor in Spite of Himself", by Molière, a handicrafts and ceramics circle, a weekly film show on a cinemascope size screen, a good library and a dance group. Next on their list is the creation of an orchestra of village children. When nothing is on, which seems a virtual impossibility, there is the Clubroom for people at loose ends, where coffee and chess are available and a piano stands inviting music lovers to play it. One of the members, Nachum Shoffman, formerly of New York, is the settlement celebrity — a pianist of concert rank.

In the summer of 1962, Kissufim was planning its Bar Mitzva celebration, commemorating thirteen years of permanent settlement. The highlight was to be a "Then and Now" exhibit stressing change and development of population and economy. Asked whether there was anything specifically American about Kissufim, one of its veterans commented: "We are a very integrated group. Perhaps the children of the Americans speak better English and do better at school. The main American impact has been in the fields of education and culture. None of the members from the United States had less than university education."

In reply to a question as to whether the issue of **lina mishpachtit** — children sleeping at home with parents — had ever arisen among the Americans or other members, another member replied, with unconcealed surprise: "The issue has never arisen here. Everyone seems perfectly satisfied with the traditional kibbutz system."

CHAPTER XIV

Urim of the Negev

When the "Hunger Road" was built by Bedouin in the days of the British Mandate, no name could have more aptly been chosen. Although the name was inspired by the dire plight of the Negev nomads who were starving during that drought year, even the landscape across which it was built amply justified the slender artery's title. Then, this part of the northwestern Negev, leading to the Gaza Strip, was a flat area with patches of wiry stubble or brush, covered with a layer of arid sand, populated only by an occasional asp or viper, and menaced by the shadow of vultures overhead.

Whatever may have been the Mandatory Government's intention, apart from providing the Bedouin with work, the thin layer of asphalt served little purpose in those days. An occasional car or truck followed its path en route to Gaza of the Philistines. The road linked no settlements. The nomads lived in clusters of black, camel-hair tents which gave them some protection from the sun. A tree by the wayside was a special treat, however gnarled its trunk or meager its shade.

The "Hunger Road" of today, in Hebrew "Kvish Haraav", winds through the shade and dusty green of growing eucalyptus trees and passes an ever-increasingly verdant carpet laid down by immigrant villages. Their houses, like white cubes of sugar rolled onto the sand, dot the countryside in growing numbers. The arching spray of sprinklers catches the flash of sunlight in a myriad of twinkling colors. About eight or nine miles down the road, proceeding south-east from the Gaza Strip is a signpost marked Urim. The kibbutz is a little off the highway whose once valid name no longer applies.

Past the entrance gate is the towering silo containing grain grown in spite of the Negev drought. It recalls the legendary message of Joseph to the Egyptian Pharaoh as he interpreted the dream about the seven fat cows followed by the seven lean. For Joseph filled Egypt's granaries with precious grain for the harsh and hungry days ahead. Perhaps these granaries looked somewhat like Urim's silo in the Negev wilderness.

To the right of the silo are the wooden bungalows and prefabricated dining hall and kitchen, the "German" type proclaiming that this is a building put up after the Reparations Agreement when payment by Bonn was made in kind. A huge lawn, shaded by trees, stretches outwards towards the permanent housing. Bordering it are the brightly colored flower beds and tidy paths, illuminated at night from tall lamp standards placed

at regular intervals. These standards are of unusual design, and they, along with the painted
refuse cans, give the site the atmosphere of a
long-established village served by an efficient
municipality.

A tour of Urim's farm confirms this impression.
The growing fruit orchards, neat green rows of
sugar beet, the white balled fluff of the cotton,
the flourishing potatoes and onions and the fields
of fodder crops all eloquently proclaim hard work
and efficient management. Of its 3,000 acres of
land, Urim by 1962 had 2,125 under cultivation.
Falcha, as the grass crops are called, accounted
for 1,250 acres, dry-farmed. The irrigated area
totalled 500 acres. The dairy had already achieved
an important place in Urim's economy, and consisted by the summer of that year of 120 milkers and
40 calves. The milkers were yielding 750,000 litres
annually, or 6,300 litres per cow. The poultry
branch had 12,000 birds, two-thirds yielding eggs,
the rest meat.

Besides its farm projects, the kibbutz had just
embarked upon a new industrial venture in the
form of a plant for producing knives. It appears
that the private enterprise "Michsaf" had not
long before gone bankrupt and the two kibbutz
villages, Nir Am and Urim, had bought up its
factory. The latter, as its share, had taken over
the knife plant and in 1962 had just started to
reorganize and reactivize its production. Further
kibbutz income was being derived from contract
work at the Dead Sea by its huge Autocar

truck. All told, total turnover of Urim in 1961
amounted to I.L.1,500,000 or $500,000, enough
— in the opinion of its secretary — "to provide
a high standard of living for a kibbutz of our
age."

This standard, in the last few years, had been
achieved by Urim at heavy cost which has included preparation for switching over from the
conventional system of housing kibbutz
children to that adopted by Gesher Haziv,
lina mishpachtit. In order to accomplish this,
Urim has had to convert one-room family units
into two-room ones, and in addition, it has had
to construct new homes of this size. The decision
was taken as early as 1958 but it took until the
summer of 1962 to implement it.

The community of the kibbutz in 1962 consisted of 140 members, 90 children (none of whom
were more than 12 years old) and two members'
parents. Eighty of the members were married
and 52 of them are of American and Canadian
origin. Five settlers are from South Africa. The
remainder of Urim's fine, young inhabitants are
pioneers from Bulgaria and Israel itself, the Sabras in the majority. The Americans were joined
by another 17 members of their movement in
October 1963, the last group of **garin aliya** in
the United States. If these newcomers remain in
Urim, exactly half of this **garin** will have achieved its pioneer goals as, so far, between 60 and
70 of its members have "passed through" the
Israel kibbutz.

In American Habonim terminology, the kibbutz
aliya is called by the movement simply **garin**
or nucleus. The first members of this second
garin, Garin Beth, arrived in Israel at
the beginning of January 1950 and went for
training to the veteran village of Geva, in the
eastern part of the Jezreel Valley.

When training at Geva was completed the
Beth vanguard in Israel had reached a strength
of eighty members. Before it was a choice of
two proposals. One was to occupy Givot Zeid,
in the western Jezreel Valley. A second was
to reinforce a Bulgarian group at Urim which was
faced with severe difficulties. It was a difficult decision to make but by the time basic training ended in September 1951 the Americans had decided
to move to Urim.

The Bulgarians at Urim had started their
group life during the dark days of World War
Two when they were rescued from Nazi Europe
by Youth Aliya and sent to the agricultural
school at Ben-Shemen. Two years later, in 1943,
they founded a settlement group of twenty members and proceeded to Ginnegar for training. By
1945 they had moved to Raanana where as an
atzmaut group they worked as day laborers. Another small group joined them at this period
following its training at Kfar Maccabi.

When in October 1946 eleven new settlement
points were established simultaneously in the
northern Negev (in answer to a British threat
to sever the region from the Jewish part of a

projected partitioned Palestine) a vanguard of the
Bulgarian group at Raanana headed for a place
called Gren, 18 miles from the present Urim site.
The night before its departure, the **atzmaut**
group at Raanana had celebrated its union with
two other groups, composed of Bulgarians with
some Sabras, and as a result, the prospective
kibbutz began with a membership of almost 100.

The original settlement site at Gren proved
to be most unsuitable for building a self-sup-
porting agricultural village. Its soil was sandy and
uncultivable. Water was scarce. The site had been
chosen by the Jewish settlement authorities at the
time because of its strategic importance, for it
was realized that war was imminent and the
Negev would be the first target of any major
Egyptian invasion. Whilst the majority of the
kibbutz remained at Raanana, those at Gren
worked primarily as hired laborers and as guards.
On August 1, 1948, the war not yet won, the
Gren group was ordered to move to a new mili-
tarily strategic point, the abandoned Arab village
of Imara.

At this village were two concrete block buildings the British had used as a police station, one
of which the kibbutz used as its first dining hall,
the other as living quarters (today it is a carpentry shop). By September 1949, the transfer
from Raanana was completed, but by this time
the kibbutz had lost 60 of its 100 members. The
main reason was that meanwhile, the parents
of many of the Bulgarians had arrived in Israel

and needed the help of their children to establish themselves in the country. Imara, by this period, was renamed Urim.

The difficulties of war, however, were not yet over for the kibbutz group. Members were still in combatant units and hence not on the settlement site. Those that were, commenced to work on the land. They started the fruit orchard, planted crops in both irrigated and waterless fields, and began to develop dairy and poultry branches. Income was supplemented in those days by wages earned in the planting of windbreaker trees for the Jewish National Fund. The carpentry shop just set up did contract work for the army and the Jewish Agency. In 1951, the Americans decided to settle at Urim as a reinforcement group and their influx made a tremendous difference to the struggling settlement.

The sudden increase in membership resulted in all agricultural branches being expanded and new ones begun. By 1952, cultivation of the unirrigated area became the major activity. Livestock was increased, the area under vegetable cultivation was extended, and a herd of sheep acquired. Americans started to assume a leading role in the economic life of the village. They also assumed a prominent place in the administration and in community activities.

The period was not without social crises in the community. The Americans, for example, were then facing their initial difficulties of adjustment to hard physical labor and integration into the

kibbutz way of life. They had trouble with the
language, climate, change of diet, and adjustment to their Bulgarian partners. It was during
this period that the Americans sustained their
heaviest losses. By the end of 1954, the severest
of these difficulties had been overcome by those
who remained. One of the problems that had not
been overcome by this date was that of security.
Marauders from the Gaza Strip constantly raided
the village, pillaging and stealing its crops, pipes
and equipment at night. For example, 10 acres of
olive saplings were uprooted and carried away.
Nearly 100 sheep were rustled from their pen.

As the farm economy developed, the lack of
manpower became a problem. The kibbutz began
looking around for further reinforcement and
made contact with a Sabra group of the local
youth movement, Hatnua Hameuchedet*. As a
result, the sixty members of this group joined
Urim after completing its training at Maayan
Baruch and Metzuba. Its members, who during
their army service became paratroopers, fought
in the Sinai Campaign of 1956 against the Egyptians, and two of them were killed in action. Of
the Sabra group, 23 were still in the kibbutz
by 1962. In 1960 and 1961 respectively two further
Sabra groups of the movement joined Urim and
together account for another 50 of the village's
current population. The remainder of Urim's 140

* Now united with Hanoar Haoved, it is called
Hanoar Haoved Vehalomed.

CHAPTER XV

Orot – Second American Moshav

Strange as it may seem, although the idea of
the small-holders' cooperative farm village was initially pioneered in Israel by the American, Eliezer Yoffe, twenty years elapsed between
the founding of Avichail and the second moshav
of settlers from the United States and Canada,
Orot. During these two decades, all the villages
settled by Americans were of the kibbutz type.
In fact, the only exception was Beth Herut, the
moshav shitufi, with its kibbutz economy and
moshav family life.

The group that started Orot, at first with the
tentative name of Beer Tuvya Beth, had a
most unusual American background. Its founders
were all Jewish farmer members of the Labor
Zionist Organization of America, who had two generations of agricultural and rural life behind them
in the region of Vineland, New Jersey.

Jewish agriculturists, many of whom concentrated on poultry-raising for eggs and meat (although a number became truck farmers as well),
first came to the United States at the end of

the 19th century as a result of the settlement
project of Baron Hirsch, a prominent French-
Jewish philanthropist. Hirsch went along with the
Zionists in so far as they stressed the over-urban
character of the Jewish people in dispersion and
the need to resettle a substantial number of them
on the land. He parted company with the Zionists as to how and where this should be achieved.
His project stressed the Argentine and United
States as places of settlement.

A strange freak of history is that Orot was
founded by the descendants of just these East
European Jews who rejected Zion for agricultural
settlement in the United States. Undoubtedly,
among pioneers in Israel kibbutz villages established by Jewish youth from the Argentine in the
last decade, are not a few who are likewise grandchildren of Hirsch's settlers. That the Vineland
group came into being in 1950 to draw up plans
to build an Israel village is unsurprising for another reason.

In Vineland, chicken-farming in particular is
becoming progressively unprofitable. The large
operators, breeding poultry on a gigantic scale,
with their huge capital and better methods, are
able to undersell the smaller man. As a result,
many of the young people of these chicken farms
are leaving the countryside for the large cities.
Moreover, whilst the grandparents may have been
adherents of Hirsch, with a firm belief in sinking
roots in the new country they chose, quite a
number of the two next generations formed and

joined branches of the American Labor Zionist Organization (Poale Zion).

Of the first fourteen New Jersey families who in 1950 enrolled for cooperative farm settlement in Israel, four today remain in Orot. They include the Weisselberg, Brodsky and Cohen families who laid the foundations not only of their village group but of an organization in the United States called Haikar Haoved, (The Working Farmer).* They sought to express the basic idea of the Israel moshav village, the self-labor of the farmer and his family, the refusal to exploit the work of others for personal enrichment. By 1953, between forty and fifty families were enrolled in Haikar Haoved, to which Orot in its early settlement days looked for reinforcement.

The original plan of Orot's founders was to establish a village of 65 American families and in its social and economic structure to follow the trail blazed by Eliezer Yoffe of Kinneret and Sam Friedlander of Avichail. Of the fifty or more families who enrolled in America, twenty actually attempted to settle at Orot, and of these exactly half succeeded. Since then, two more families from the United States and three from Canada have joined them, and this brings to 15 the grand total of tried and tested American and

* Now functions in the western world as the Israel cooperative settlement movement — Tnuat Hamoshavim.

Canadian families in Orot in 1962. They include
a few members of Habonim who changed their
minds about kibbutz life, and several Habonim
families who recently came directly to Orot from
the United States.

As the foundation group at Orot realized that
its population turnover was high and that it
urgently needed new reinforcements, it modified
its original conception of an all-American village
to one populated by settlers from English-speaking countries. As a result, 15 families from South
Africa, 4 from England and 1 from Australia
joined. With so strong a nucleus from the west-
tern world, and with land available for further
expansion, Orot further broadened its concepts.
There are today 14 non-English-speaking families in the village, accounting for its total number of 49 families and farms.

The village, its housing divided into three
distinct sections of 20, 19 and 10 farm units, will
not further expand. Although, at the beginning,
the target was 65 families, the settlers have since
decided that this would have made each individual
farm much too small to be workable. To ensure
viability of each holding, they increased the land
area available to it and fixed a population ceiling
at 49 families, apart from 7 others who are employed in the village services and not as farmers.
Each family started with $4\frac{1}{2}$ acres of land, received $4\frac{1}{4}$ acres more, and in addition owns $1\frac{1}{2}$ acres
of a cooperatively-worked citrus plantation. As of
1963, all of Orot's land is under irrigation.

In the ten years of its existence, Orot's economy as a whole has progressed rapidly. For example, in 1961, the village produced 870,000 litres of milk and 1,500,000 eggs, reaching the limit set by the Ministry of Agriculture to ensure profitability in both of these branches. These limits are set to avoid over-production and decline in prices on a national scale. Villages are thus given "quotas" on the basis of which they obtain feed for livestock at carefully controlled prices to encourage production. Another index of Orot's progress is that of its 49 farms, 30 by 1962 had reached solvency, that is they were paying their way and even beginning to repay the settlement loans they had taken.

These debts are of course based on settlement loans in the form of first livestock, farm buildings, seed, irrigation piping, and other equipment. They are obtained from the Settlement Department of the Jewish Agency and, in the case of Orot, from the land development company, ICA, as well. Regarding many of these farms, investment by the settler now equals in value that first made through loans. There is, however, an unevenness of development within Orot, as in other moshav villages, the result of differences in the ability, size, devotion and luck of each family. Whereas solvency was already achieved by some farmers after five years, others have taken ten and some will need more. Average annual turnover of the farms is between I.L.20,000 and I.L.24,000 or $6,666 and $8,000.

The dairy branches of individual farms at Orot reflect these differences. Some have 3 or 5 cows, others rear cattle for meat as well. Whilst most farmers, apart from their share in the common citrus plantation, grow fruit trees (peaches seem to be both successful and profitable) there are differences in how they use their land. For example, the Brodsky family, Yaakov from Vineland, Riva from Winnipeg, concentrate on seedlings — pepper, tomatoes, cauliflower and cabbage in season — "because this requires no large financial investment." They produce 200,000 seedlings per month and sell one-half to three-quarters of them at I.L.7 to I.L.10 per 1,000. They are helped, after school hours, by Malka, aged twelve, and Sari, ten, their two daughters. No doubt when Gershon, now just four, is old enough, he too will pitch in.

Light-haired Yaakov Brodsky is blessed in a special way in his children, because two of them are girls. Had all of them been boys, the oldest would inherit the family farm, the others would have to seek land or other vocations outside. This is a moshav problem as a whole — the kibbutz, with its collective economy, does not face it, at least not in the same way. When the number of kibbutz children is too large to be absorbed fully by the farm economy, this type of village seeks a solution in developing an auxiliary industrial enterprise that provides additional employment possibilities. The moshav with its private farmers it at a disadvantage. The large families of Oriental farmers often force them into

cutting up the farms into smaller units for their
sons, with the result that none of the subdivisions
is large enough to support a family. The only solution, according to Brodsky, is to be sure of
keeping the farm intact and in the possession
of one, or at most, two families only (i. e., partnership with the oldest son).

In Orot, morale is high. There is no backsli-
ding, no occasions when cooperative farmers sell
part of their produce privately, by-passing the
cooperative treasury. "We have no sales outside,"
emphasizes the village treasurer, "all marketing is
through the cooperative." The village has passed
beyond the stage of "natural selection". Those
who could not adjust to farm and rural life left
Orot during its first decade; those that
remain today have durable roots in their soil.

Not all the profit made by the farmers is
returned to them by the cooperative in cash. The
amount handed over each month is determined
by the size of the family and the level fixed at
the General Meeting, held once per month. The
sum of I.L.100 monthly, for example, is held
back in payment of taxes from which the village provides educational, social, health, administrative and other services, and repays its building loans, taken to finance investment of public
institutions. Whilst families draw between I.L.400
and I.L.500 monthly, their real incomes are between I.L.600 and I.L.700 when the value of
services and the amount of food each grows for
family consumption are taken into account. For

a village 10 years old, this is considered a high standard of living.

Pride of Orot so far, among its central institutions, it its handsome Beth Haam* (Community Center), which is more than a mere meeting hall. Built as a square, enclosing a central lawn, flower beds and trees, this patio-style structure includes an assembly hall for 300 people, a synagogue, offices, club rooms and other facilities. It is of modern, simple and striking design, its outer wall of hollow, open gray brick. The village store, called the **tsorchaniya,** is run on a non-profit basis by an American family that gave up farming. Not far from the Beth Haam, playing fields are being developed for the younger generation. They have not yet been completed as they await funds.

One of Orot's financial problems, its shortage of cash to complete its building program, is due to the limited size of the village population. It takes longer to raise large sums by taxing only 49 families than in the case of larger moshav communities. One of the consequences is that Orot has not yet managed to build a swimming pool of its own and hopes that neighboring Beer Tuvya will in the meantime offer its facilities. The older village has a pool of Olympic size. Another shortage felt by Orot is its lack of a Guest House, as the village has more

---

* The Beth Haam was built with financial aid of the Histadrut Campaign of New Jersey.

visitors than its inhabitants can accommodate. "This," says the treasurer, "will have to be built by a private investor."

Parents in Orot pay no fees for education of their children. From the age of 3 to 5, the village supports the kindergarten; from 5 to 14, the government provides the budget under the Education Act of 1949, and from 14 until the end of high school, Orot pays out of village taxes. After that age, the family must find its own budget for university or specialized training. There are 127 children in the village, 24 of them babies, 22 in kindergarten, 70 in elementary school, 5 in high school, 3 in the army, 5 now full members of the community and 3 others married. The elementary school to which Orot's children go is at Kfar Warburg and is shared by the five villages: Orot, Beer Tuvya, Avigdor, Timorim and Kfar Warburg.

Housing in Orot has, from the very first, been of higher standard than any new moshav-type village since 1948. At the beginning, as a result of a special allowance by the Jewish Agency matched by the same amount from each family — four-room family units were erected to make initial settlement easier.

Cultural life in the village is far from organized. In 1962, according to one member, "the only group activity, besides the monthly General Meeting, is the weekly cinema performance." Although this cultural passivity, at least on an organized plane, is a negative feature of its life, Orot's constant success as a pioneer venture can certain-

ly not be questioned. The Vineland farmers, unlike their grandparents before them, have established a permanent settlement this time. The difference is that they became farmers in a
land which needed a permanent peasantry and
among a people in the process of building a culture
on its newly redeemed land.

* * *

One of the villages that sends its children
to the same elementary school as does Orot is
Timorim started in southern Judea in 1954 as
a moshav shitufi by a group of South Africans.
Among its founders were, originally, 12 Americans
and Canadians of whom 11 remain today. The
village was established by members of the youth
group Hanoar Hatzioni of the United Zionist Party
of South Africa.

Houses in Timorim are unusual, original and
attractive, with slanting red-tiled roofs forming
an interesting pattern. All of them are three-room
family units. The village, holding 1,000 acres of
land, grows cotton, vegetables, seedlings, and grass
crops, has dairy and poultry branches and produces
steel furniture, shelving, and solar water-heaters.

In 1962, members of the village did not antici-
pate that any reinforcement group from the
United States would join Timorim. Its population
was growing slowly, families joining it singly as
a result of personal contacts. Whilst not an American settlement point, nor the product of a
pioneer nucleus from the United States, Timorim—

like many other villages in Israel—includes its
small number of American pioneers.*

Today, Timorim remembers it has Americans.
In ten or twenty years it will have forgotten their
origin, for a pioneer village makes its Hebrew
culture the daily fare of its life and ethnic characteristics of members recede into history.

*See Appendix.

CHAPTER VII

Galon – Nachshon – Hazorea

On the fringe of the Lachish region, which lies at the junction of Southern Judea and the Northern Negev plain, is a kibbutz of Hashomer Hatzair called Galon. It is next door to Kibbutz Beth Guvrin, in Arabic Bet Jibrin, a hotly contested prize in the battle between Israelis and Egyptians in 1949. In fact when Galon itself was first settled, as one of 11 villages established in the region in 1947, it was part of a protective shield designed by Jewish settlement and defense authorities at the time to stop an invader from the south.

The other villages of this shield became famous battle-scarred landmarks of Israel's War of Independence. They are Yad Mordechai, Negba and Gat which halted mass Egyptian attacks led by tanks and preceded by artillery and aerial bombardment. Galon, less known, played its own special part in halting the offensive. It was assaulted from the east by strong Egyptian units and so sure were the local Arabs of success, they followed Farouk's army into the field with sacks to pick up the expected loot. Galon disappointed them. Its electric mines stopped the tanks at its outer fence. Its rifles and machine guns mowed down Egyptian infantry. The attackers withdrew and, before they could return, the new Israel Defense Army swept south and pushed them into a pocket at Faluja.

The small group that started Galon in 1947 consisted of 20 young Polish immigrants, the last members of Hashomer Hatzair to escape from Europe before the outbreak of World War Two. They were the vanguard of a **kibbutz aliya** of 100 members that had gathered at the moshava (private village) of Ness Ziona and were earning their living in local orange groves and at building as any typical **atzmaut** group. When their permanent settlement site was given to them, the men began transferring to it with the knowledge that foundations of their village would have to be laid under war-time conditions. Only when hostilities ended did the completion of transfer take place, the last to arrive being of course the mothers and children.

Meanwhile, another type of transfer was taking place in and from Europe. Most of the original Polish group had been trapped there in 1939 and few survived. Twenty, however, had fought or worked in the Soviet Union until 1944. Among them was Mordechai Rossman, leader and hero of the refugees of the famous ship Exodus. As soon as the Germans were driven back over the Russian frontier and westwards towards their own, Rossman and his friends began organizing the rescue operation of Jews called the **bricha,**

which smuggled them out of Soviet territory to
Italy and France for departure on the "illegal"
ships to Palestine. Hence Rossman and the other
nineteen survivors of their **kibbutz aliya** reached
Galon just after the war.

Three years after the Polish group began settlement at Galon, the first Americans who were
to become their partners arrived at Merhavia for
pre-settlement training. A second nucleus went to
Dalya for one year They were members of Kibbutz Aliya Zayin, in their movement's history
the generation that followed Kibbutz Barkai. In
the United States "Zayin" had consisted of 120
people but by the time it gathered on its
Israel site this number had declined to less than
80. It took eight years for the 80 to assemble
at Galon which is quite a normal process for such
a youth movement group as its departure from
Hashomer Hatzair in America had to be staggered
until younger people were ready to take over the
educational work with junior groups.

During their training period, when the proposal was made that they should reinforce Galon,
the Americans conducted a prolonged and, at
times, sharp discussion with the executive body
of their settlement federation, Kibbutz Artzi. The
latter proposed union with the Galon group because the European war had destroyed its manpower reserves, whilst its economic and community development required such immediate expansion.

One of the Americans a decade later summed

up the feelings of his group at the time when he commented: "When we came here, we were more than 70 people. We did not want to be here. All wanted to be where there were younger people." The "united" kibbutz began as two distinct groups and has continued in that state ever since. After work hours, both live very much to themselves, and are in fact integrated only until four o'clock.

To the outsider, such a development may seem inconceivable in view of the close knit nature of collective life. It is true that in addition to building a settlement together, two groups may be jointly involved in organized cultural and other activities, as well as in common meetings and decisions of the General Meeting. But, in a kibbutz sense, this is insufficient for organic integration. An age gap of 15 years is both unusual and almost impossible to bridge, particularly when it is reinforced by other such differences as background, culture, outlook and approach.

Several differences in approach between Poles and Americans manifested themselves at times. The American girls, for example, had to fight for their right to work in the farm branches and not be restricted to the maintenance and educational services. This is an important issue in terms of kibbutz ideology for the collective bases its claim to real equality between the sexes upon their fullest partnership in the economic aspects of its life. All work, according to kibbutz philosophy, has equal social usefulness but, psychologically, it does not necessarily have the same value.

When the Americans turned the concrete square outside the kibbutz dining hall into a roller-skating rink, this, too, emphasized the gap. The Poles were in fact slightly bewildered. Nor did they share in the baseball craze of their partners who were soon playing outside teams from the Canadian and American embassies. The way the Americans like to spend their annual vacations is another case in point. The Poles traditionally spend the holiday in one of the Rest Centers (Batei Havraa) of the Histadrut Health Service, Kupat Holim. Asked why the Americans don't follow suit, one American replied: "Which American ever heard of spending his summer vacation in a Beth Havraa or in visiting other kibbutzim? Rachel and I took our I.L.70 per head, plus traveling expenses and went to Eilat — we had much more fun."

Recently, Galon has been reinforced by a group of Sabras from the Israel section of Hashomer Hatzair. Together with the first of the kibbutz-born children to be demobilized from the army, this Sabra group numbers 70 members. Most of them are around 20 years of age, about 10 years younger than the 45 Americans of Galon today. If only for reasons of age (and there are other reasons as well), it is likely that the Americans will remain apart during their leisure hours.

The Americans of Galon are most active in the village's cultural life, particularly in its dramatic group, choir and orchestra. At present pre-

paring their version of the opera "Porgy and
Bess", they have already successfully put on Arthur Miller's "The Crucible", and "Charlie's Aunt".
The swimming pool, financed in part by the father
of one of the American members, in part from
German Reparations money, adds to everyone's
enjoyment. In terms of organization, Galon is a
success.

This is most evident from its economy which,
since 1947, has made rapid and most gratifying
progress. Out of a total area of 3,750 acres,
the farm has 200 under irrigation. It grows cotton, barley, vegetables, fruit and citrus, has 250
acres of pasture for its 600 head of sheep, and
devotes the rest to grass crops. Its dairy houses
60 milkers, its poultry section 12,000 birds which
laid until recently 400,000 eggs per year. The
egg quota has been cut, under the Ministry of
Agriculture plan, and the kibbutz objects as it be-
lieves Negev settlements should have preferential
and different treatment.

Besides agricultural branches, Galon has a factory producing electric fans which it purchased
from a private owner. It also has a drop-forge,
run "by the only man in Israel who has the skill
to work it, a member called Eliezer who was sent
to Germany and England for training." This forge
is producing hoes and hammers. The factory now
employs 20 people and, in addition to its profitability, "provides work for those more than 45
years old who find it difficult to continue   in
agriculture".

Besides its 140 members, to which the 70 newcomers must be added, Galon has 189 children,
60 of whom are at school, and 20 in the army.
It has also a group of 25 trainees of Youth
Aliya. As in all kibbutzim, hopes of complete social integration are confidently vested in
this younger generation. When they inherit the
kibbutz as a new generation of born and bred
farmers, memories of the distinctiveness and difference of parents will belong to the family album.

* * *

Nachshon

Whilst other Zionist movements in America
may claim to have sent to Israel as many individual pioneers, Hashomer Hatzair is indubitably
ahead in the number of villages its groups have
founded. With almost clock-like regularity, its
senior age groups in the United States have
formed a **kibbutz aliya** every two years and sent
their settlement groups across the world to Israel. Beginning with Ein Hashofet and Kfar Menachem, the American chain has grown by the
addition of links like Hatzor, Ein Dor, Barkai,
Sasa and Galon.

The McCarthy witch-hunt, however, which
struck fear into the hearts of the palest pink
leftists, created an atmosphere that was injurious
to Hashomer Hatzair. Although its socialism had
no direct application to the American scene, parents of children became more than concerned
and as a result the movement began its numeric-

al decline. Naturally, this in turn had an adverse effect on the morale of its senior members.

Besides these special problems of its left-wing ideology, Hashomer Hatzair faced a problem that all the other pioneer youth movements were confronted with in the United States. The affluent environment generated no social idealism and robbed young people of exhuberance. From early age life became cut and dried, particularly among the Jewish middle and upper middle class. All headed for college and university, careers were mapped out in the early teens. Patterns of life and culture were set, with prestige dating, the two-car family, status symbolism, graduation and early marriage. Amid this pressure of conformism, which considered anything original to be maladjusted, children began losing their spontaneity, one of the preconditions of youth movement growth.

Besides this internal development, external affairs had their influence. Socialism, of any kind, became identified in the American mind with Russian and Chinese communism. Democracy, it was wrongly held, was irreconcilable with socialism. The success of American capitalism in providing both high living standards and freedom, in contrast with the Stalin dictatorship and its treatment of its own and subject peoples, together provided "convincing" arguments against all left-wing movements. On the Jewish front, the State of Israel had been won, its gates were open to all oppressed and unwanted Jews. American Jew-

ry, integrated and prospering in a multi-ethnic
environment, had, historically, no need to move
to Israel. To help Israel — certainly! To live
there — this was a question of choice, and of
course, for the very limited idealistic or "maladjusted" few.

This mixture of subjective and objective reasons made life for Hashomer Hatzair extremely
difficult. A new generation has grown up since
McCarthy, which is showing signs of wanting to
work things out for itself. It is no longer satisfied with the black-and-white puritanism of its
predecessors. It may well be that within an environment of reawakened intellectual curiosity,
a new lease on life is to be given to the youth
movements as well. The condition, of course, is
that they too learn to live with the new, in Israel
as well as the United States.

Be all this as it may, the generation of American Hashomer Hatzair that followed Galon was
the first to produce a failure in the field of settlement in Israel. Out of 40 of its trainees dis-
patched to Kibbutz Nachshon, about half the number sent to previous settlement groups, 3 remained by 1962. In the past, Hashomer Hatzair's **kibbutz aliya** in America consisted of 100/120 members, and by the time it gathered in Israel, it
settled with 70/80, which was considered a normal
and viable settlement group. However, the
forty members of Kibbutz Aliya Het who
reached Nachshon were so few because of the
decline of the movement in the United States.

That these forty members of the **kibbutz aliya**
failed in Israel was not merely because of
their limited numbers. It was also partly due
to deficiencies in their education and movement
background in the United States. It is symptomatic
that of the 37 who left Nachshon, all without
exception made no attempt to settle in Israel's
towns, old or new. Instead, they returned to their
country of origin. As they left the kibbutz between 1955 and 1960, a period of tremendous
development in the country and of profound change
for the better in its overall standard of life, this
cannot be explained away by **tsena,** the local
word for austerity (or, by extension, scarcity).

Nachshon, a kibbutz in the Jerusalem Corri-
dor and less than a mile from Latrun in Jordan, was founded as a border strongpoint in
1950. It was started by 60 Sabras of the Israel
youth movement who were reinforced three years
later by 15 Polish pioneers. The Americans arrived in 1954/55, the same year that 20 South
African members of Hashomer Hatzair joined the
village. Since then, in 1957 and 1962 Nachshon
has received two further Sabra reinforcement
groups of 80 and 40 respectively. Out of all
these groups, its membership on November 30,
1962 totalled 105. On that date it had 53 children.

Nachshon, it must be admitted, had no easy
settlement, and this is proved by its appearance
after twelve years of existence. Three factors
have been responsible for the slowness of its

development compared with other kibbutz villages of the same age and period. They have been: the rocky, hilly nature of much of its terrain; the problem and cost of its water; and the unstable nature of its settlement groups, a factor undoubtedly influenced by the economic handicaps produced by the first two. On its total area of 1,250 acres of land, Nachshon by 1962 had cultivated 25 acres of apples, 50 acres of cotton, 50 acres of vegetables, 7.5 acres of apricots, peaches and grapes under irrigation and, on the rest, was growing grass crops by dry farming. It was about to add 50 acres of citrus.

To supplement its farm economy, Nachshon has developed three sizable livestock branches. It has a large herd of cattle, totalling 350 head, all of which are being raised for beef. It has 400 head of sheep for which ample grazing ground exists in the surrounding hills. Its large poultry section produced over 1,000,000 eggs in 1961. In fact that year was the first since establishment that Nachshon could show a profit on its balance sheet, a sum of I.L.88,000 ($29,333). Its turnover had reached I.L.800,000 ($266,666). Water, that year, was costing Nachshon 13 agorot* (equivalent to about 4 cents) per cubic meter, compared with 3 agorot paid by villages in other parts of the country. This higher price is due to the higher cost of bringing water from afar to such a height, and many believe the difference should be borne by the government.

* Plural of agora, one hundred of which equal one Israeli pound, called lira.

As noted earlier, the Americans from the outset had never been a strong group, either numer-
ically or ideologically. In contrast, they found
their Sabra partners who had settled Nachshon's
site a tough and close-knit group. The Israelis
had served together in the same military unit
through the War of Independence and had got
used to roughing it. They had also got so used
to each other that when their new and young
American partners arrived they made little effort
to absorb them socially.

In consequence, the Americans lived by themselves after work hours, except for organized kibbutz activity. "The Sabras never invited us to
their rooms," one of the Americans complained.
The complaint is somewhat misleading. In America it would appear to be an instance of uninhib-
ited misanthropism. In Israel, it would have a
different interpretation. Sabras are often casual
and don't stand on ceremony. They expect people
to drop in uninvited. If they don't, the Sabra
suspects lack of interest. Obviously, what was
missing was an attempt on both sides to understand differences in tradition and values and
adjust accordingly.

This mistake in approach by the Sabras had
more serious manifestations. They maintained
their hold on the administrative and leading positions of the kibbutz and made no attempt to introduce the Americans to any of them. This contrasts strongly with the attitude of the Sabras
of Hatzor in its early days who were careful to

develop a sense of "parity" so that the Americans felt the kibbutz was as much theirs.

The Sabras had of course good grounds for complaint on their side. They were all excellent workers and had a lot of stamina. The Americans could not compete. The Sabras accepted fully the kibbutz educational system of children. The American mothers, although they handed their babies over to the nurses of the creche, complained a lot about the standard of nursing and the conditions. Whether justified or not in this or that detail, it was clear that underneath their criticism was a basic reluctance to have other people look after their children.

Food was another bone of contention. The drop in standards for the Americans was severe. The accent on "vegetables for breakfast and at dinner" became monotonous and a source of complaint. They wanted a more varied diet, not always limited by budgetary considerations. Nor did impoliteness on the part of the Sabras make matters any easier. Few ever thought it worthwhile to greet the Americans with **boker tov** (good morning). Not all Sabras are so contemptuous of such niceties, but those who are often don't appreciate their importance and in Nachshon — things being what they were — this added fuel to the fire of American discontent. For these and other reasons, all but three left Nachshon.

Today, some years later, the Sabras at Nachshon admit to many mistakes in their relations with the American group. Some of these mistakes

were due more to the youthfulness and inexperi-
ence of the Sabras than to any inherent characteristics. Moreover, in part, their estimate of
their partners in terms of work and preparedness
for kibbutz life was essentially correct. The tra-
gedy was that the Sabras were both unable and
unwilling to be more patient in their approach
and extend themselves more to help the Americans change themselves.

The fact that all of the Americans who left
Nachshon made no attempt to resettle elsewhere
in Israel is itself an indication of their poor morale. In all fairness, however, one of their difficulties should be understood. It is a problem that
has faced many pioneers from youth movements
outside Israel who, on deciding to leave their kibbutz villages, find it hard to live elsewhere   in
the country.

Many members of the movement did not complete their education in their countries of origin.
Their movements decided that higher study was
incompatible with pioneer life. People who had
degrees, the movements at one time believed,
would be reluctant to become or remain farmers.
Hence, on leaving the kibbutz late, they were un-
equipped for the outside world. They were unpre-
pared to become hired laborers, unskilled and
"exploited", in private enterprise. Only kibbutz
ideology could induce them to enter such occupations. Possibilities of training for professions or
as skilled artisans are much better in the United
States and entail much less hardship. Moreover,

in many instances, after western immigrants decide to leave the kibbutz, their families are prepared to help them train vocationally to earn their livelihood outside of Israel. No such family help is available to them in Israel where they are on their own. Only the most determined are prepared to stay in Israel and fight this problem out.

There is another problem for the ex-kibbutz member. There are various agencies from which he can obtain housing loans. Loans, however, have to be repaid and the struggle to make ends meet and repay these loans simultaneously makes living standards low for some years at the beginning of resettlement. It is more than tempting under these circumstances to return to America or England, sometimes even with the sincere intention of coming back to Israel with training and a little capital. Few make the second journey. By the time they have such training and a little capital most have passed the age of 30 and more, their children have become integrated in their new environment, and the idea of beginning life again under Israeli conditions becomes more and more unenchanting.

* * *

Hazorea

As a result of the Nachshon experience, the members of the next and current **kibbutz aliya** of American Hashomer Hatzair were of the view that they should establish a kibbutz of their own

in Israel. They did not want to join one already
settled as a completion or reinforcement group.
Nevertheless, when the first nucleus of "Tet"
reached Israel and proceeded to Kibbutz Zikim
for pre-settlement training, its members were per-
suaded by the Kibbutz Artzi federation to which
they belonged to join Kibbutz Hazorea, a veteran
village. Thus, on completing their year at Zikim,
the 18 members of the "Tet" group arrived at
Hazorea in the summer of 1962.

The choice of Hazorea for this most recent
group from American Hashomer cannot of course
be compared to Nachshon. The former village is
well developed economically and has more mature
members. Its living standard is high, its facilities
for vocational training and absorption of new
members extensive in kibbutz terms. Hazorea, for
example, in addition to its thriving farm, has
two flourishing factories. One is a substantial
furniture producing enterprise, one of the largest in Israel. It already represents an investment of $25,000 and is now to be tripled in size
with the aid of a Government loan and private
Dutch capital. The second kibbutz factory is a
plastic plant in which $100,000 has so far been
invested.

The farm economy of Hazorea, based on 1,875
acres of land, now includes 200 acres of fruit
orchards, 107.5 acres of carp-breeding ponds, 150
acres of pasture, 400 acres of field crops and
such profitable products as melons and sugar
beet. It has dairy and poultry branches, an en-

gineering shop, garage and other developed services. The kibbutz has just built a beautiful dining hall, has a swimming pool and an interesting museum. Its standard of housing is high, its landscaping very attractive.

Hazorea is famous in the kibbutz movement and country as a whole for its successful cultural achievements. Many of its members are highly talented, particularly in the fields of music and art. Socially, the Americans should have a wide choice, in their own and in other age groups. For among Hazorea's children are many of their own age. By the end of 1962, its population numbered 320 members, 240 children, 40 members' parents and various training groups. Other members of Kibbutz Aliya Tet are expected to join the American nucleus there.

Hashomer Hatzair of the United States is following this pattern set by "Tet". The current group is going to Barkai.

CHAPTER XVII

Religion and Labor

"We have no Rabbi and we need one... he could work half day in agriculture and the remainder teaching. We want to apply Rabbinical teachings to the sphere of work according to Halachic principles as set down by the Rabbinical authorities." This was the view of Eli Klein, member of the kibbutz village of Shluchot in the Jordan Valley, one of a chain of religious collectives called Hakibbutz Hadati. This tall, kind and earnest young man from New York is a graduate of the Orthodox pioneer youth movement of America, Bnei Akiva. Together with 18 others from the United States he has remained and integrated well in the life of Shluchot, a village so beautiful it won in 1956 the Ministry of Agriculture's national prize for landscaping.

The American group at the village started to arrive in 1954 and when fully gathered there numbered originally 35 members. Of the 16 members who have since left Shluchot, seven are in another village called Beerot Yitzchak, the remainder returned to the United States — but a

few who did so immigrated a second time and
now live in Israel cities. According to Eli, there
are in the country almost 250 graduates of the
American youth movement Bnei Akiva and about
35 live in kibbutz villages. When interviewed in
the summer of 1962, he added that a new group
of 10 trainees from America was expected at Tirat Zvi in the near future and that, annually,
about 40 members of the movement were immig-
rating to Israel.

The group at Shluchot is therefore the largest
kibbutz nucleus Bnei Akiva has today in Israel.
The thirty other members in this type of village
include 11 in Tirat Zvi, 9 in Yavne, 5 in Saad,
the rest in twos and ones elsewhere. Over 200
members of the movement are settled in towns,
apart from a group of 15 families who established a particular type of rural suburb called Beth
Hazon near the large moshav of Kfar Haroeh in
the Hefer Valley. Most of the people of this
rural suburb were once members of the first kibbutz group ever established by Bnei Akiva in
Israel, a nucleus at the village of Kfar Darom
that numbered 60 people but soon broke up.

Bnei Akiva started in the United States as an
outgrowth of a religious youth organization called Hashomer Hadati — The Religious Guard —
which began in 1934. During the first five years
of its existence, Hashomer Hadati tried to find its
identity. In general, its members consisted of Orthodox youth who believed not only in Zionism but
also in the ideals of labor within that broad na-

tional movement. Not content with mere support of these national, religious and labor principles, they sought ways of expressing them in their own daily lives. In 1939, just before the outbreak of World War Two, Hashomer Hadati decided to convert itself into a religious pioneer youth movement and changed its name to Bnei Akiva, after the famous Rabbi who together with Bar Kochba led the last Judean revolt against the Romans from 132 to 135 C.E.

Both the Zionist and labor principles of the new movement were inspired by its religious beliefs. To its members, the only type of Jewish State that could justify its existence would be one based on the values of the Bible and Rabbinic Law. These values, however, according to Bnei Akiva, were best and most truly expressed in the Biblical period by the social prophets, Isaiah, Jeremiah, Amos and others. These prophets had called for a society based on social justice, equality and the sanctity of the individual. Hence, to Bnei Akiva, the kibbutz type of village in Israel most closely represented in its daily life the practical expression of this Biblical socialism.

Bnei Akiva in America, and as a youth movement elsewhere in the Western world, summed up its ideology in the two words **torah** (scriptures) **veavoda** (labor), and established training farms to prepare those of its members who had committed themselves to religious kibbutz life. Others, unwilling to live collectively, decided to migrate to Israel and settle in cooperative villages or as workers in the towns. The first training farm of the movement in the United States was purchased in 1940. It was at Cranbury, New Jersey.

It was not until 1947, however, that the first group of trainees of the movement left for Israel. It established itself at Ein Hanatziv in the Beisan Valley for a year of pre-settlement preparation and in March 1949 its 60 members decided to unite with South Africans and the survivors of the destroyed village of Kfar Darom and together establish a new settlement point. Thus began the Orthodox kibbutz of Netivot Morasha on a site near Kibbutz Yavne in Southern Judea.

The original Kfar Darom group, graduates of Youth Aliya who had once made frontpage news as the first Jewish children to be brought out of the smoldering ruins of Nazi Europe through Teheran, had in 1947 occupied a frontline settlement site south of Gaza as one of 11 such groups. When the Egyptian army drove northwards in 1948, Kfar Darom stood directly in its path and met its full-scale assault. For weeks, the youngsters of the new settlement stopped massed armored and infantry assaults. Over ten thousand shells were pumped into their village until almost everything was razed to the ground. They were cut off and when ammunition for their light weapons and most other supplies ran low, they received military orders to withdraw and fight their way back to Israel lines. Reluctantly, they obeyed and what was left standing of their encampment was completely destroyed when it was over-run by the invaders. The 50 survivors of this epic struggle united with the Americans and South Africans.

The union did not work out. By 1951, 50 out of the original 60 Americans had left the kibbutz. One of those who left, and later settled at Beth Hazon, summed up her memories of this experience: "In my opinion, the Kfar Darom group were young and enough of them had a warped outlook because of the bad times they had had to set the tone for the rest. Not only had their village been destroyed by the Egyptians. It should be remembered that these people as children had survived the bestiality of Hitler's Europe, their families and homes were destroyed, they were deprived of stability, education and background." Considering all that, it is a wonder that having emerged from such a nightmare they had the capacity to establish a pioneer collective, itself a testimony that they had regained much of their faith in man, and defend it with such valor.

Nevertheless, this does not mean that the past had not left its scars. The American, quoted above, continued. "They (the Kfar Darom people) looked upon us Americans as 'rich'. For example, my father worked all his life for a wage and we were far from wealthy. But, in their eyes, we had had so much more and they

were jealous of the relative comfort and security of our past. Not all of them were like this, but enough to make life tense and unhappy. Some of their group were not even 20 years old whilst we were in the mid 20's; this, too, made a difference."

Like all such experiences, that of the American Kfar Darom group was by no means one-sided, in kibbutz terms. The American women, for example, never really accepted the idea of kibbutz education and separate sleeping quarters for the children. Their partners "without kids of their own" would not hear of any other system. It may also be assumed that when it came to work and the preparedness to live under difficult material conditions — inevitable for any young kibbutz — the Kfar Darom people must have had a clear edge. As the 50 Americans left the settlement but one year after the union, the trial period was most certainly too short for either side to be sure that the union was impossible.

It is of interest that the Kfar Darom group has recently decided to become a moshav shitufi village maintaining its kibbutz economy but with its families living as in a moshav. Undoubtedly, had that decision been taken at the time the Americans were there, many of them would have remained in the kibbutz. The village, since reinforced by groups from Egypt and Israel itself, has meanwhile done well economically and is considered a successful community. Not one of the Americans had remained there by 1962. Most stayed in Israel, almost all who had families.

The Kfar Darom experience generated a discussion in American Bnei Akiva reminiscent of that which had earlier taken place in American Habonim. It revolved around the issue as to whether future groups should constitute large nuclei in Israel to establish new villages or whether they should in small numbers be absorbed by well-established settlements. The 35 members who left in 1954 for Shluchot had decided to follow the latter course. In the words of Eli Klein: "We don't want too many Americans in one place because of the Kfar Darom experience."

Shluchot itself, three miles from Beth Shan, a modern immigrant town on the site of an archaeological treasure trove, is one of a bloc (**gush** in Hebrew) of four Kibbutz Hadati villages. The others are: Tirat Zvi, Sde Eliyahu and Ein Hanatziv. Its settlement day was July 10, 1948, in the midst of war and Arab invasion. The first settlers, 50 graduates of Youth Aliya who came from Yugoslavia, Germany, Holland, and Belgium in 1943/4, had been at Sde Yaakov as an **atzmaut** group. They were given 1,250 acres of hot and dusty land in the valley, a tough settlement site with little water available.

In the fourteen years of Shluchot's existence its community has grown to 120 members and 120 children (the oldest now 17). In 1962, it had in addition 25 candidates for membership,

5 members' parents, a group of trainees of Aliyat Hanoar, and an intensive Hebrew course
(ulpan) for 35 immigrants from North Africa
and Eastern Europe. Its economy by that date
included 150 acres of fishponds, 30 of vineyards,
125 of citrus, 30 of other fruit and the remainder
of field crops grown under dry-farming conditions. In addition, the village had 200 head of
cattle, half of which were milkers, and 14,000 poultry for both eggs and meat.

Supplementing its essentially agricultural economy, Shluchot — together with the three other
religious collectives of the bloc — has invested
as a partner in a number of regional enterprises.
These include the local cotton gin, first in the
country, which is directed by a member of Kibbutz Ein Hanatziv; a date-drying plant; a poultry-
processing enterprise; a drying plant for grass
crops (falcha); and a citrus processing enterprise, now nearing completion. Shluchot, in addition to holding shares in these profitable ven-
tures, also provides some of their labor. It also
shares in a regional school with its three partners.

The Americans at Shluchot have integrated
successfully into its economic and social life.
One of them — a graduate of Yeshiva University, New York — now leads the field crop
branch. Another is engaged in fruit experi-
mentation and is doing research at the Beth
Yerach station. Another American is responsible
for the magnificent landscaping which has won

Shluchot such merited national acclaim. One of its features is the attractive pool for toddlers surrounded by green shade trees, lawns, neat hedgerows and flowers. It is astonishing to see this luxuriant and exotic growth in the midst of a tropical dust-bowl.

As a religious collective, based on **torah veavoda,** Shluchot has many unique features. Like all settlements of the Kibbutz Hadati chain, its community seeks to reinterpret traditional values in the setting of a modern Jewish society. For example, in the days of ancient Judea, land was left fallow each seventh year. Shluchot, and similar villages, today grapple with the problem of reintroducing the Sabbatical Year without damaging their economies. "Perhaps the solution may be found in hydroponics," says Eli Klein. One of the goals sought, in leaving the land fallow on the seventh year, is to provide a Sabbatical year of study and meditation for the workers released from labor.

Another problem of the religious kibbutz has been how to keep the Sabbath as a day of rest when cows have to be milked. On the one hand, as is well known, it is injurious to the animals not to milk them. To do so, however, means not only someone violating Sabbath laws but also wasting the milk, for if milk obtained on the Sabbath is sold this would represent a second violation. The solution to both problems was found. Mechanical milking, started by automatic clocks, obviated the need for most labor. The follow-

ing day the milk was transformed into cheese at
the local Tnuva dairy plant.

Not all such problems, however, have been
solved. Animals, as well as humans, have to be
fed on the Sabbath, hence some people must
work. This matter is handled as in any kibbutz:
people take turns doing unavoidable Sabbath work,
and each member's turn comes around about once
in four weeks. The point is that these young Orthodox Jews are faced with problems others have
been able to avoid for the last two thousand
years. For as long as the Jew lived dispersed a-
mong non-Jews, public services could be maintained
by the latter. For example, a Jew could rest
comfortably in his home on the Sabbath with the
knowledge that if fire should break out or a
burglar attempt to enter, non-Jewish firemen
and police could be called. In an all-Jewish society, this is no longer possible, there are only
Jews to man such services.

In other words, with the return to Zion, the
Jew is faced with the problem of a religious revolution and not merely reform. For the first
time since dispersion he must begin to apply his
spiritual values to the practical life of his own
sovereign community. In the Diaspora his Judaism
could be comfortably confined to the realm of
prayer and ritual. Here, in Israel, as in the days
of the Bible, he must find a new unity between
spiritual and practical man. The religious kibbutz, in pure form, underlines the broader problem
of Israel as a state that is specifically Jewish.

Barnett went to the Jewish National Fund
in Jerusalem seeking to lease land for an American group near the village and after protracted
negotiations, and the help of the A.A.C.I. National Office, he was successful. Dividing the land
into plots on which houses could be built and sizable vegetable gardens or orchards planted for
each family, Novick and Barnett were flooded
with applications from the ex-members of Kfar
Darom and other American immigrants. Building
began in 1952 and good mortgages were obtained
from the Settlement Department of the Jewish
Agency. Most of the money for each home, however, had to be found by the applicants themselves, a problem made easier by the then fledgling
A.A.C.I. which took its compatriots under its wing
and aided them in their dealings with the Jewish
Agency as well as in finding mortgage money.
Thus, Beth Hazon became the first A.A.C.I.-aided
housing scheme and was the forerunner of such
other A.A.C.I. developments as Nayot in Jerusalem.

The houses built consisted of four rooms, a
kitchen and bathroom and have around them a
quarter acre of land for fruit trees and vegetable
garden. The fifteen families, plus eight others who
were living on the site in huts before the Americans came and who joined their project, pay taxes
to Kfar Haroeh for light, water, educational, medical and other services. The twenty-three families elect their own management committee,
Vaad Hashechuna, which is responsible for the
special needs and activities of their suburb, but

they also take part in the life of Kfar Haroeh.
For example, their children go to its schools and
belong to its local groups of Bnei Akiva.

The Beth Hazon suburb has its own local store,
run by one of its families, Goldstein of Philadelphia. It is building its own community synagogue
and center to cost about $10,000. When a new-
comer seeks to join Beth Hazon, the community
as a whole decides whether or not to accept him.
If it does, the new family is allocated a fine plot
on which to build its home. The suburb has also
its own social and cultural committee which dis-
cusses problems and decides on programs of activity. For example, during Hanuka and Purim,
the adults have huge parties for which they prepare a full two months beforehand and to which
come hundreds of visitors, many of whom were
either members of Bnei Akiva in America or of
the Kfar Darom group. Naturally, special celeb-
rations are organized for the children. Another
adult activity is the Bible study circle which is
well attended and successful.

Life at Beth Hazon runs very smoothly today.
This was not always the case. At the beginning,
in particular, there were difficulties. Esther Barnett of New York, wife of David who initiated
the idea, says: "We were the first outsiders.
People of Kfar Haroeh did not understand what
Americans were doing here. They only understood that people came to the country who were
chased out of other lands. By now, they have got
used to us and the idea that Americans can

choose to live in Israel voluntarily. As we were
all from Orthodox homes and maintained our
religious observance this made it possible for us
to find common ground and establish good relations. The fact that the level of Hebrew knowledge of the Americans was high also helped a
great deal."

A second problem at first was relations with
the eight families already living on the suburban
site. The Americans had to induce them to share
responsibility for developing the suburb as a
whole. Though they worked well for themselves,
these families were far from interested in projects the Americans considered essential to
make everyone's life easier. For example, roads
and street-lighting had to be introduced. However, the eight families accepted the idea of dem-
ocratically-taken community decisions and cooper-
ated. The decision to build a separate synagogue
and community center has also been accepted by
them.

Why the synagogue? Because the regular
Kfar Haroeh synagogue lacked adequate pews
for women to participate in the services. The
Americans, used to having their wives attend
either in the balcony or in a separate, curtained
area, couldn't accept a synagogue which made
almost no provision for them.

Of the American families, all of whom have
4 or 5 children, the women work full time in
their households and share in tending gardens and
fruit trees. The men are employed as teachers in

Kfar Haroeh's two main educational institutions of high school standard, one academic, the other vocational, and in two other professions. A breakdown of their occupations revealed that 2 are engineers, 2 are Rabbis, 2 are vocational instructors, 6 are teachers, 1 is a shopkeeper, 1 a veterinarian and the fifteenth, the secretary of a village nearby called Kfar Yedidya. The Beth Hazon community has a cooperatively-owned lemon orchard, worked by hired hands.

Esther Barnett sums up life in Beth Hazon as follows: "Most of us are not interested in city life. I can do nicely without window shopping. It is wonderful here for the children as they are safe and free. They have lots of kids of Kfar Haroeh to play with. We are at the same time a closed community with its own point of view and no conflicts arise among us. We have our own harmonious social life, there is a high degree of cooperation between people and we have all the advantages of a kibbutz without its hardships. We could never have the life in a town we share at Beth Hazon. We don't have to dress up, and hence feel at ease. In short, we are very happy here."

The contrast between the two stable and settled groups of American Bnei Akiva at Shluchot and Beth Hazon is sharp and vast. They have in common the happiness of living a fully Orthodox life on holy soil and of building, each in his own way, a religious society on the land in Israel. Although their movement's emphasis is on pioneering, and the kibbutz form of life will in the future be stressed in its educational group, members will continue to come and enter the varied types of Israeli farm villages. This is likewise true of the other pioneer movements in the United States — Habonim, Hashomer Hatzair and Hechalutz Hatzair. There will be some failures, but there will be many successes.

In the more than three decades of American pioneering in Israel it has been the kibbutz type of village which has dominated its record of success. True, the moshav and moshav shitufi, and other forms of rural settlement, have made a substantial contribution to the record but the kibbutz in Israel is undoubtedly so far the most intense, undiluted and truest expression of its national, social and ethical values. There are some who dispute this claim, or who are of the view that whilst the kibbutz fulfilled so worthy a role in Israel's formative days, new objective needs require new and different forms of pioneering. Whilst this may be partially true, as long as Israel has open and dangerous borders and man strives for justice and brotherhood, the kibbutz will remain both a necessity and a challenge.

Undoubtedly, young Jewish men and women of the West will continue to respond. Those seeking other forms of pioneering, yet wishing to take part in the creative adventure of rebuilding a land, people and culture, will choose other types of settlement, both rural and urban.

CHAPTER XVIII

Summing Up

Since Sam Friedlander built his lone house
in the northern Sharon Plain, over a thousand
Americans and Canadians have settled permanently as pioneers in various parts of Israel. Most of
them came and remained in groups, 60% of them
chose the kibbutz type of village as the most
desirable form of life. There is, unfortunately,
no precise, or even approximate, figure as to
how many young people from the North American continent have passed through pioneer villages to settle permanently in Israel's towns and
cities. The number by far exceeds that of the
people who remained in the villages. It is not surprising. Pioneering, particularly of the kibbutz
type, demands such willingness to sacrifice and
such consistent strength of character that only
the fittest persevere.

Some four hundred Americans and Canadians
have settled privately on the land in Israel. And
their contribution, as exemplified by citrus "king"
Mendes Sacks, is considerable. The accent upon
kibbutz in no way detracts from their pioneer

value and importance, or from that of the American and Canadian moshav and moshav shitufi. Their achievements are not less. However, whilst these latter types of village are an offshoot of the western pioneer youth movements, the kibbutz idea has been the major trend.

This is particularly true of the first five years in the existence of new villages when conditions are most exacting and the individual is faced by the greatest challenge. It is during this period that young kibbutz nuclei sustain their heaviest losses.

About the relatively small community of 1,424 American and Canadian rural pioneers (5,000 including families) certain definite conclusions can be drawn. According to the most recent figures of the Association of American and Canadian Settlers in Israel (Hitachdut Olei America Vecanada Beyisrael), there are 15,000 settlers of all types in Israel from the North American continent. The pioneers therefore represent 10% of that total, somewhat less than the national average. On the other hand their number in kibbutz type villages soars well above it. Less than one-third of all Israelis engaged in mixed farming live in kibbutzim; sixty percent of Americans and Canadians in agriculture do so.

It is true that all kibbutz villages, regardless of differences in ideology and in origin of population, share the same fundamentals. It is equally true, though, that they differ in personality, as do individuals. Kibbutzim which have been founded and settled by strong groups from America and

Canada have distinctive traits, often discernible
in their external appearance, usually apparent in
the nature and expression of their community
existence. Nevertheless, in spite of these similari-
ties, they differ somewhat from each other. Such
differences, between kibbutz villages of the same
movement, reflect the contrast between successive
generations.

In kibbutz after kibbutz visited by the author,
American and Canadian members insisted that
in their fusion with groups from other countries
they had played a conspicuously liberalizing role.
In this, there was no difference between the villages of Hashomer Hatzair, Habonim and other
movements. Whilst accepting the same concepts of
social responsibility and discipline as their partners — whether East European or Sabra — the
Americans and Canadians had never lost sight
of the individual and his profound personal
needs and aspirations.

There are reasons, of course, for this greater
emphasis upon respect for individual rights and
aspirations. These are to be found in their background and not in ideological or political differences. The Americans and Canadians of such
kibbutzim had behind them a past richer
and more experienced in democracy and civic
rights. Neither the East European nor the Sabra
had a comparable background nor did they possess
all the self-confidence which centuries of
such freedom produces. Whilst the East European
and Sabra often tend to take a more extreme

position, the American listens more readily to the other point of view. He is more prepared to compromise, is more relaxed about ideas.

This pronounced liberalism manifests itself in another way. The kibbutz movement in Israel has already had many years of successful experience. As in most revolutionary societies, its achievements led to profound conservatism. Young kibbutz villages tend to accept unquestioningly the experience of their predecessors. In those where strong American and Canadian groups have played a significant role, however, there is more questioning, a greater tendency to be inventive and to introduce change. The reintroduction by Gesher Haziv, and later by other American Habonim villages, of the system **lina mishpachtit** first met with strong opposition from their parent federation. Despite this, these kibbutzim persisted and demonstrated the advantages of the system. Though not universally copied, **lina mishpachtit** has at least been accepted.

This tendency to introduce change has not restricted itself to education. In American villages it has manifested itself in economic and technical things. Many of the auxiliary industrial enterprises introduced reflect directly the know-how and scientific training brought over from the North American continent. Similarly, an emphasis on better sanitation and hygienic conditions, an insistence on more aesthetic landscaping, a greater variation in diet, a better variety and quality in clothing, more attractive club rooms and many other such improvements may often be traced in such mixed "ethnic" kibbutz communities to their American and Canadian members.

Even within the political life of settlements of the Hashomer Hatzair chain can this specific influence be felt. The pioneers from the West, long before Khrushchev's revelations about Stalin and his regime at the 50th Congress of the Russian Communist Party, were among the most sceptical and critical in all evaluations of Russia and the world Communist line. Many of the things they said in their early days in the youth movement even before settling in Israel have become accepted and commonplace in their Israel party, Mapam, in the last few years.

Many more examples of this sort can be cited. All of them point to a specific Western tradition. There are other differences, not less apparent. One is the fact that a high percentage of Americans and Canadians have come from large cities and are the products of their sophistication. The small-town backgrounds of some of their East European partners, and the limited experience of the Sabras, often produced parochial points of view and dogmatic reactions. This contrast is often intensified by the fact that a high percentage of the Western pioneers are college and university graduates whilst their partners have often stopped their formal education at high school.

Since World War II the cultural gap between Western and European partners has often been

wider still. Many of the youth who survived the
Hitler holocaust were not only deprived of formal education in elementary and secondary school.
They also, in considerable number, had never
known the love, warmth and security of normal
family existence. This, naturally, influenced attitudes towards education and family life in their
kibbutz community. Moreover, the savage conditions which such young people survived in Europe sometimes left a residue of bitterness, tough-
ness and insensitivity that had inevitably to af-
fect the quality of their kibbutz life. At times
these factors have produced sharp tensions and
clashes in the mixed groups where Americans
and Canadians have been partners.

In quite a different way have contrasts revealed themselves between Americans and Canadians,
on the one hand, and Sabras on the other hand.
The Western pioneer is a Zionist by choice, the
Israeli by birth. The former tends to be romantic, the Sabra essentially practical. The Sabra
enjoys the advantage of Hebrew as his mother
tongue. The American or Canadian has an endless struggle to master the language. In addition,
the Western pioneer faces such problems as ac-
climatization, a violent change in living standards
from a comfortable middle-class existence to one
of hard, manual toil. Even when the Israeli
moves from urban to rural pioneer life his decline
in living standards is far less.

This relative contrast in material background
and idealistic motivation, together with the dif-

ference in preparedness between Western and native pioneers, often produces sharp difficulties and tensions, particularly at the beginning of American-Sabra unions. The western group may find itself in the position of a junior and dependent partner, a situation scarcely improved by the fact that its academic and intellectual level may be higher than that of the Sabra group. The latter may also be more homogeneous, having fought and lived together before settlement in the same army unit; as a result, it may also be more immediately adjustable to the primitive and hard conditions of a new kibbutz encampment.

For these and other reasons the record of American and Canadian pioneer groups has not always been one of success. There have been failures, as in the case of Hasolelim, Nachshon and Kfar Darom, although these are in the minority. From both success and failure, however, it is possible to conclude that there are certain essential preconditions for the successful acculturation of American and Canadian pioneers within the context of mixed "ethnic" communities. In many respects these preconditions may be compared to the essential ingredients of successful marriage between individuals.

Differences in themselves are neither a positive nor negative attribute. In the case of union between two strong personalities they add color and variety and hence enrich the partnership. When the union consists of two unequal parts, or two weak partners, such differences can con-

tribute towards failure. Such is the case with
kibbutz partnerships as well as that of individuals. A Western group, lacking in Hebrew knowledge, without sufficient training vocationally, its
members insufficiently toughened for hard physical work, may bring a decisive weakness into
a kibbutz partnership. Experience has demonstrated that people leave kibbutzim because the
going is tough, simply because it is hard to be
a pioneer, and not because they cannot get on
with Poles or Sabras.

There are of course many rationalizations.
People rarely admit weakness and failure and
seek to justify their abandonment of the pioneer
life by blaming others. In their heart of hearts
they know that these are not the true reasons.
Often the differences are minor, but may be the
straws that break the camel's back. Most Americans and Canadians consulted in the preparation
of this book agreed that the process of creation
itself in building a new village and its society
and common basic idealistic motivations are sufficient to guarantee that groups of requisite
strength and training will successfully unite into
a single unit, regardless of dissimilarity in background.

The most successful kibbutz villages have
been the product of such unions. No pioneer
youth movement in America has yet succeeded
in building a kibbutz solely of its own members.
It is doubtful whether the concept should be en-
couraged. The first village to put it to the test

was Sasa, although its experience because of particularly difficult settlement conditions may be considered inconclusive. Nevertheless, the major argument against the "uni-national" American and Canadian village is that whilst it may succeed in a material sense, its prospects of cultural integration are less than those of mixed groups. Such villages tend to become English-speaking islands in a Hebrew sea.

There are, theoretically, equally valid reasons for rejecting the view that Western pioneers should integrate as individuals or tiny groups into already established villages. To establish a new point of settlement provides infinitely more satisfaction and fulfillment to the pioneer. The process binds him more profoundly to both soil and community — he is more directly and actively involved. Moreover, the youth movement from which the pioneer graduates, derives far greater benefit educationally and otherwise from the Israel village of its own creation. Until the establishment of Kfar Blum and Gesher Haziv, the effectiveness of American Habonim was impaired because its pioneers were lost to it through their individual settlement in veteran villages such as Afikim, Degania Beth, Ramat Yochanan and others.

The problem, however, is not merely theoretical. One of the consequences of decline in membership of all the pioneer youth movements in the Western world has been the dispatch of groups in the last few years too weak quantitatively and qualitatively to embark upon the establishment of new settlement points. The small nucleus of Americans at Hazorea is an example of this development. The creation of a **kibbutz** or **garin aliya** in the United States depends upon the availability of over 100 members at the start. Experience has shown that such large groups usually begin in America with 150 people, reach Israel with 100 and in Israel after sustaining losses during the first years of settlement, consolidate at 50 to 70.

It is questionable whether the American movements will ever again attain the numbers which will make possible such nuclei of 150 members. The answer does not merely depend upon developments on the American scene. Pioneering in Israel itself is undergoing a process of basic change. As a result, there are people who question the very future of the kibbutz movement. Yesterday, they say, the worker was the "aristocrat" of Zionist settlement as he was in short supply and had to be created by the voluntary act of déclassement of middle class Jewish youth from abroad. Now with the mass immigration of Jews from North Africa and the Middle East, all of whom arrived without capital in Israel, the majority of the population have become workers by necessity and the aura of "aristocracy of labor" has receded.

The kibbutz as a society, however, is more than an association of individual workers. It is also a concept of life based upon social equality,

pioneering and defense. It still has a vital role
to play in the settlement of the most difficult
areas in the country yet awaiting pioneer development. It still presents a challenge to all other
forms of life in terms of human values. It is
precisely these values which in the past have
attracted Western youth so much to kibbutz
pioneering. The question is, however, whether the
far-reaching changes which have in the last five
years taken place in Western youth, and for that
matter in Sabra youth as well, are likely to cause
a fresh wave of idealism. Without such idealism
the youth movements cannot grow.

Yet, both in Americans and Israelis there are
many signs of just such an idealistic development. People often mistakenly believe that de-
pressed social conditions are responsible for the
growth of idealistic forces. More often than not
they lead to despair and reaction. There are
many indications that idealism is bred by moral
and ethical revolt against the corrupting influences of material satiation. This is particularly true of youth who are usually the first to
revolt against the double standards and injustice
of the older generation.

It is by no means inevitable, however, that
an idealistic resurgence must necessarily produce new people for the kibbutz movement in
Israel. They may choose instead settlement in the
Negev development towns, or find satisfaction
in providing Israel with a stream of highly quali-
fied and skilled technicians and professionals.

One cannot be dogmatic about so fluid and dynamic a society as Israel's. Nor can one predict with any degree of certainty the trends within American and Canadian Jewries in the next decade. Much depends upon the quality and depth of Jewish consciousness and education in both these countries and the nature of Israel's impact upon their Jewish communities.

Suffice it to say at this juncture that the first thousand American and Canadian pioneers who have ventured, tried and succeeded in Israel have established their place in that country's history. Their example is an inspiration which the communities from which they came must surely cherish. Nor should it be forgotten that those who first lived in a village and then settled elsewhere in Israel have also make a valuable contribution to the upbuilding of the land.

ABOUT THE AUTHOR

Yaakov Morris, Irish-born diplomat and author, was Israel's consul in New York from 1957 to 1961. Before entering Israel's diplomatic service, Yaakov Morris headed the section for English-speaking countries of the Youth and Hechalutz Department of the World Zionist Organization and in that capacity, was responsible for contacts with the pioneer and other Zionist youth organizations and their settlers in Israel. He is at present on loan from the Israel Ministry for Foreign Affairs to the Jewish Agency for Israel as the latter's Treasurer for the United States, Canada and Central America.

Yaakov Morris wrote and edited a number of books, including "Pioneers from the West" (W.Z.O. Jerusalem) and "Israel's Struggle for Peace" F. M. Publications). His latest work, for which David Ben Gurion wrote a special intrduction, is "Masters of the Desert — 6,000 Years in the Negev" (G. P. Putnam's Sons, New York).

TABLE I — THE NUMBER OF AMERCANS AND CANADIANS IN AGRICULTURE ACCORDING TO SETTLEMENTS, 1962

A. Hakibbutz Haartzi

Ein Hashofet	65
Kfar Menachem	25
Hatzor	31
Ein Dor	42
Sasa	30
Barkai	53
Nachshon	3
Galon	45
Hazorea	14
Hamaapil	2
Mishmar Haemek	6
Beth Alfa	4
Gaash	3
Lehavot Habashan	4
Negba	3
Nirim	4
Ein Hachoresh	4
Admit	1
Gaaton	1
Gat	1
Dalya	1
Yassur	2
Megido	2
Mesilot	1
Metzer	1
Merhavia	2
Nachshonim	1
Nir David	2
Ein Shemer	1
Ramat Hashofet	1
Shoval	2
Shaar Hagolan	1
Shaar Haamakim	1
Davir	1
	360

B. Ihud Hakvutzot Vehakibbutzim

Degania Beth	17
Afikim	14
Ramat Yochanan	12
Kfar Blum	50
Maayan Baruch	7
Gesher Haziv	70
Urim	52
Enat	3
Mishmarot	1
Hatserim	1
Geva	6
Kfar Giladi	5
Maayan Zvi	5
Maale Hachamisha	3
Kfar Maccabi	1
Netser Sereni	3
Degania Aleph	1
Hamadia	1
Kfar Hanassi	1
Ginnegar	2
Kvutzat Shiller	1
Beth Haemek	1
Tel Yosef	4
Ein Gedi	2
Ayelet Hashachar	2
Metzuba	1
Ramat David	2
Sde Boker	1
Mishmar Hasharon	1
Ein Harod	1
Hanita	1
Yiftach	2
Nahal Oz	2
Zerahya	1
Ein Gev	1
Kinneret	2
	280

TABLE I — (Continued)

C. Hakibbutz Hameuchad

Kissufim	39
Givat Brenner	4
Revivim	6
Naan	2
Maagan Michael	7
Hulata	2
Beth Hashita	3
Beth Keshet	1
Hagoshrim	5
Sdot Yam	7
Gadot	6
Givat Chaim	4
Afek	2
Givat Hashlosha	1
Gevat	2
	91

D. Hanoar Hatzioni

Hasolelim	7

E. Hakibbutz Hadati

Beerot Yitzchak	1
Tirat Zvi	11
Yavne	9
Lavi	2
Saad	5
Ein Tsurim	2
Sde Eliyahu	2
Shluchot	19
	51

F. Moshavim

Timorim	11
Avichail	12
Tsofit	12
Beth Herut	60
Orot	32
Kfar Malal	7
Nir Banim	4
Nahalal	5
Beth Hever	1
Shadmot Devora	2
Kfar Monash	10
Kfar Vitkin	3
Rishpon	2
Avigdor	4
Negba	4
Kfar Yehoshua	1
Beer Tuvya	2
Dor	1
Tarshicha	1
Moshav Habonim	12
Lahish	4
Bizra	1
Kfar Hess	2
Kfar Yehezkel	2
Ein Iron	2
Kidron	2
Ramat Zvi	2
Beth Yitzchak	2
Beth Yannai	6
Bustan Hagalil	1
Bnei Tzion	2
Ein Vered	2
Even Yehuda	2
Ilanot	1
Ein Vered	2
	239

DISTRIBUTION OF AMERICANS AND
CANADIANS IN AGRICULTURE, 1962

Kibbutzim	789
Moshavim and Moshavim Shitufiim	239
Private Agriculture	400
TOTAL	**1428**

This figure refers to active adults. If children and dependents are included, there are 5,000 individuals from the United States and Canada in agricultural settlements in Israel.

LIST OF SETTLEMENTS

(Numbers indicate position on map)

1. Avichail
2. Ein Hashofet
3. Kfar Menachem
4. Kfar Blum
5. Beth Herut
6. Hatzor
7. Ein Dor
8. Gesher Haziv
9. Sasa
10. Barkai
11. Hasolelim
12. Yiftach
13. Kissufim
14. Urim
15. Orot
17. Nachshon
18. Hazorea
16. Galon
19. Shluchot
20. Beth Hazon

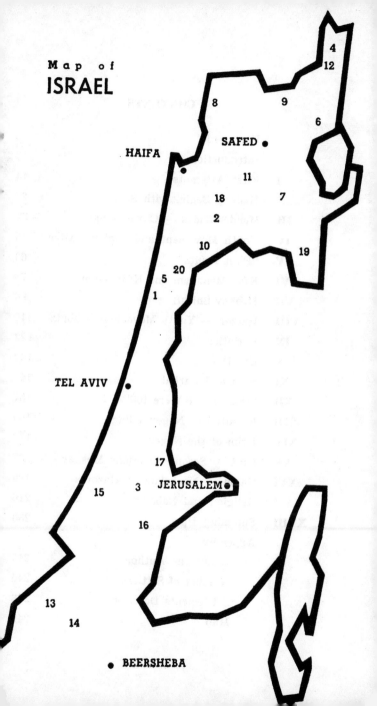

Map of
ISRAEL

4
12
8   9
6
HAIFA   SAFED
11
18   7
2
10   19
20
5
1
TEL AVIV
17
3   JERUSALEM
16
15
13
14
BEERSHEBA

CONTENTS